P9-CMT-672

ULTIMATE
Explorer
FIELD GUIDE

Rocks
&Minerals

Nancy Honovich

NATIONAL GEOGRAPHIC
WASHINGTON, D.C.

Contents

SANDSTONE pg 141

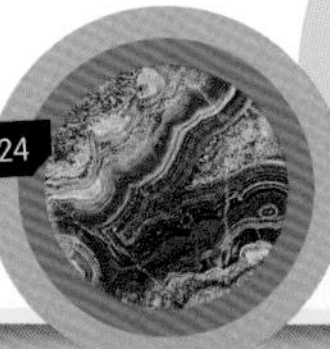

AGATE pg 24

LET'S GO Rock Hunting!

From the cliffs of California's Yosemite National Park to the miles of sand found on Florida's beaches, rocks and minerals are all around us! Geologists have discovered thousands of different types of rocks and minerals over the years, and people have come up with some pretty cool things to do with them, including making tools, fashioning jewelry, building structures, and extracting metals. So how can you tell one rock or mineral from another? Well, that's what this guide is all about. With it you'll get detailed descriptions of some of the most important rocks and minerals that make up our world. Dig in and become an expert rock hound!

HOW TO USE THIS BOOK

GUIDEBOOK ENTRIES Get outside and look around. Rocks are everywhere, and many of them have minerals that you see or use every day. Use the specially designed entries in this guide to help you find them and discover cool things about them. Callouts from the pages below and at the right will help you get started.

HERE'S THE COMMON NAME FOR THE ROCK OR MINERAL.

THIS VITAL INFO FOR MINERALS INCLUDES THE CHEMICAL FORMULA, COLOR, HARDNESS, CLEAVAGE, FRACTURE, STREAK, AND LUSTER. LEARN HOW TO DECODE THESE TERMS ON PAGES 12 AND 13. ROCK VITALS INCLUDE GRAIN SIZE, MAJOR MINERALS, MINOR MINERALS, TEXTURE, ORGANIC MATTER, AND STRUCTURE. DISCOVER THESE TERMS ON PAGE 115.

GET THE BASICS ON EVERY MINERAL AND ROCK, FROM WHERE IT FORMS TO WHAT YOU SHOULD LOOK FOR.

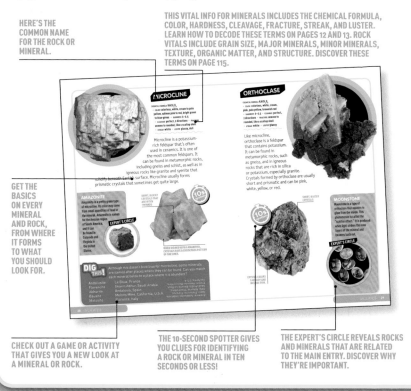

CHECK OUT A GAME OR ACTIVITY THAT GIVES YOU A NEW LOOK AT A MINERAL OR ROCK.

THE 10-SECOND SPOTTER GIVES YOU CLUES FOR IDENTIFYING A ROCK OR MINERAL IN TEN SECONDS OR LESS!

THE EXPERT'S CIRCLE REVEALS ROCKS AND MINERALS THAT ARE RELATED TO THE MAIN ENTRY. DISCOVER WHY THEY'RE IMPORTANT.

ROCK STARS These special feature spreads focus on information about a unique grouping of minerals or rocks.

ON EACH SPECIAL SPREAD, TEXT BLOCKS REVEAL WHAT YOU MIGHT FIND IF YOU LOOK CLOSELY AT ROCKS AND ROCK FORMATIONS. FOR INSTANCE, YOU CAN USUALLY FIND DINOSAUR BONES ONLY IN SEDIMENTARY ROCKS.

YOU'LL SEE CLOSE-UP PHOTOGRAPHS OF DINOSAURS, GEMSTONES, BIRTHSTONES, AND FOSSILS.

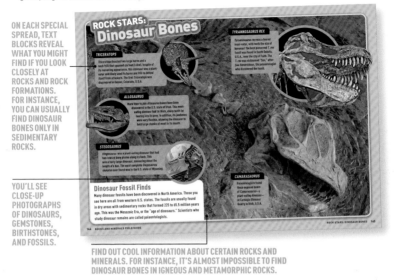

FIND OUT COOL INFORMATION ABOUT CERTAIN ROCKS AND MINERALS. FOR INSTANCE, IT'S ALMOST IMPOSSIBLE TO FIND DINOSAUR BONES IN IGNEOUS AND METAMORPHIC ROCKS.

ROCK GROUPS You'll find that scientists classify minerals into various groups, based on their chemical makeup. This system of classification helps scientists study the differences and similarities between minerals. Tabs at the bottom of each page give you the name of the group.

WHERE DID THAT NAME COME FROM? FIND OUT HERE!

A TAB NAMES THIS MINERAL GROUP: SULFIDES, SULFATES, AND SULFOSALTS.

DISCOVER FUN INSIDE STORIES ON THE ENTRY.

YES—MINERALS AND ROCKS CAN BE FUNNY!

THE WHOLE WORLD Rocks

Rocks are everywhere! We're not just talking about the pebbles in a stream or stones on a hiking trail. All of Earth's surface is covered by rock. That includes every mountain, hill, island, and continent! What's even cooler is that if you take all the water out of the ocean, you know what's left? You got it—rock!

What Is a Rock?

A rock is a naturally occurring solid object made mostly from minerals that can be grouped into one of the following categories: sedimentary, metamorphic, and igneous. These categories are determined by the way in which a rock forms. Sedimentary rocks, like shale, form from pieces of other rocks. Igneous rocks form when hot liquid rock cools. Metamorphic rocks form when intense heat and pressure cause a rock to change.

SHALE

What Is a Mineral?

Minerals are solid, nonliving substances that occur in nature. Each type of mineral has its own chemical composition and structure. Minerals are the basic components of most rocks. Some rocks, like quartzite, are made of only one mineral, while others, like granite, are made of many different minerals. By studying the minerals that make up a rock, scientists can learn important information about Earth.

GRANITE

AMBER

When Is a Rock NOT a Mineral?

Not all rocks are made of minerals. Coal is a rock that's made from plant material, while amber is made from ancient tree sap. Since plant material and tree sap come from living things, they aren't considered minerals.

Tools
OF THE TRADE

Every good rock hound knows that when it comes to collecting—and examining—rocks and minerals, having a set of tools on hand is key. Here are a few:

Hammer and chisel: A hammer and chisel will help you break a large rock apart.

Goggles and gloves: When hammering, little bits of rocks can go flying everywhere. So always wear goggles or safety glasses to protect your eyes and gloves to protect your hands.

Sieve: A sieve is an ideal tool for sifting out mineral fragments in loose gravel.

Bucket: You'll need a bucket to carry the rocks that you find. If you don't have a bucket, a sturdy backpack works, too.

Stiff brush: A stiff brush will help you clean any debris from your rocks.

Bottle of vinegar: A bottle of vinegar can help you determine what a rock is made of. For example, rocks that contain the mineral calcite will fizz when acid is poured on them.

Field guide: Use a good field guide—like this one!—to identify the rocks you collect.

Writing materials: It's always a good idea to have a notepad and pen or pencil to take notes when you're in the field.

Camera: Sometimes a rock is too big to take with you. Taking a picture can often help you get an idea of how the rock formed.

Minerals: A CLOSER LOOK

Geologists have identified thousands of different minerals on Earth. These minerals come in a wide variety of shapes, colors, and textures—and can be used to make many different things. For example, galena is used to make lead, and gypsum is used to make plaster.

But what exactly makes a mineral ... a mineral? Scientists have identified five characteristics that all minerals must have:

1. **A mineral must be a solid**. In other words, liquids and gases are not considered minerals.

2. **A mineral must occur naturally on Earth.** That means that materials such as plastics, which are made by humans, are not minerals.

3. **A mineral cannot come from or be made by a living thing.** Objects such as pearls, which are produced by oysters and other shelled mollusks, are not minerals. The same applies to corals, which are organisms that live in the water.

4. **A mineral must have an unchanging chemical formula.** Don't worry—this isn't as tricky as it sounds. All minerals are made of one or more chemical elements, such as oxygen, sodium, and chlorine. Each type of mineral is made of a specific combination of elements. For example, halite is a mineral that consists of sodium and chlorine. Its chemical formula is NaCl; "Na" represents sodium, while "Cl" represents chlorine.

Dig This!

Throughout this book, you'll see a chemical formula for each mineral. You can use the table below to help decode the elements in each formula:

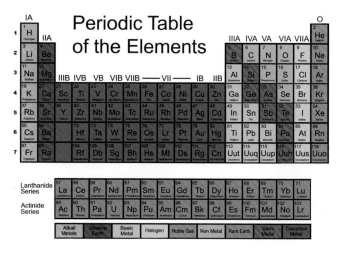

5. **A mineral must have atoms arranged in an orderly crystal structure.** Everything in the world is made of tiny units called atoms. When atoms join together to make a specific mineral, they usually form some type of crystal. The atoms in the crystals of the same mineral are always arranged in the same pattern.

Crystals Have Habits!

In addition, the crystals may have a unique habit or shape. For example, some crystals may look like cubes, while others look like long columns. Here are a few crystal habits you'll see in this book:

Prismatic: long in one direction, with well-developed faces
Columnar: long in one direction and resembling a long, rounded column
Bladed: Long and flat, like a blade
Fibrous: threadlike
Granular: small and grainlike

VANADINITE

PRISMATIC

COLUMNAR

GRANULAR

Identifying Minerals

With so many different minerals in the world, it can be a challenge to tell one from another. Fortunately, each mineral has physical characteristics that geologists and amateur rock collectors use to tell them apart.

Identifying Minerals

Check out the physical characteristics below: Color, Luster, Streak, Cleavage, Fracture, and Hardness. These can help you tell quickly which mineral is which.

AZURITE

Luster

"Luster" refers to the way light reflects from the surface of a mineral. Does yours appear metallic, like gold or silver? Or is it pearly like orpiment or brilliant like diamond? "Earthy," "glassy," "silky," and "dull" are a few other terms used to describe luster.

ORPIMENT

DIAMOND

FLUORITE

Color

When you look at a mineral, the first thing you see is its color. In some miner-als, this is a key factor because their colors are almost always the same. For example, azurite, above, is always blue. But in other cases, impurities can change the natural color of a mineral. For instance, fluorite, above, can be green, red, violet, and other colors as well. The change makes it a chal-lenge to identify by color alone.

Streak

The "streak" is the color of the mineral's powder. When minerals are ground into powder, they often have a differ-ent color than when they are in crystal form. For example, the mineral pyrite usually looks gold, but when it is rubbed against a ceramic tile called a "streak plate," the mark it leaves is black.

PYRITE

Cleavage

"Cleavage" describes the way a mineral breaks. Since the structure of a specific mineral is always the same, it tends to break in the same pattern. Not all minerals have cleavage, but the minerals that do have cleavage, like this microcline, break evenly in one or more directions. These minerals are usually described as having "perfect cleavage." But if the break isn't smooth and clean, cleavage can be considered "good" or "poor."

MICROCLINE

GOLD

Fracture

Some minerals, such as gold, do not break with cleavage. Instead, geologists say that they "fracture." There are different types of fractures, and depending on the mineral, the fracture may be described as jagged, splintery, even, or uneven.

Hardness

The level of ease or difficulty with which a mineral can be scratched refers to its "hardness." Hardness is measured using a special chart called the Mohs Hardness Scale. The Mohs scale goes from 1 to 10. Softer minerals, which appear on the lower end of the scale, can be scratched by the harder minerals on the upper end of the scale.

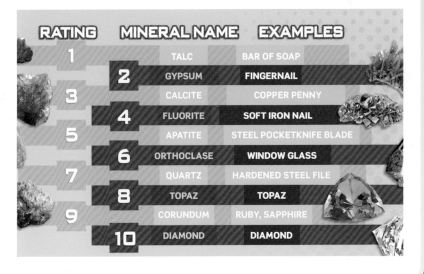

RATING	MINERAL NAME	EXAMPLES
1	TALC	BAR OF SOAP
2	GYPSUM	FINGERNAIL
3	CALCITE	COPPER PENNY
4	FLUORITE	SOFT IRON NAIL
5	APATITE	STEEL POCKETKNIFE BLADE
6	ORTHOCLASE	WINDOW GLASS
7	QUARTZ	HARDENED STEEL FILE
8	TOPAZ	TOPAZ
9	CORUNDUM	RUBY, SAPPHIRE
10	DIAMOND	DIAMOND

Mineral Groups

Scientists classify minerals into various groups that are based on each mineral's chemical makeup. This system of classification helps scientists study the differences and similarities between minerals.

Native Elements

Native elements are minerals that are made of only one element. Generally, there are three types of native elements: metals, such as gold; semimetals, such as graphite; and nonmetals, such as sulfur.

SULFUR

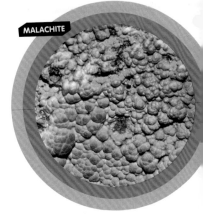

MALACHITE

chemical formulas. This unit, called the carbonate radical, then combines with one or more metals to form a carbonate mineral. For example, when the carbonate radical combines with copper, the result is a green mineral called malachite, which can be used as a gemstone.

Silicates

MICROCLINE

Silicates are the largest known group of minerals. They make up 95 percent of Earth's crust and upper mantle. All silicates contain silicon and oxygen. However, different silicates can contain other elements as well. For example, microcline feldspar is a silicate that contains potassium and aluminum, in addition to silicon and oxygen.

Carbonates

Carbonates all contain one carbon atom and three oxygen atoms in their

Oxides

When oxygen is combined with one or more metals, an oxide is formed. The minerals in this group vary in hardness. They also come in many colors, ranging from white and gray to pink and ruby red. Hematite is an example of an oxide that's formed when oxygen combines with iron.

HEMATITE

GOETHITE

GYPSUM

Sulfates

Sulfates are minerals that contain a chemical unit called the sulfate radical, which is made from the element and four oxygen atoms joined together. Sulfates usually occur near Earth's surface. One of the most common sulfate minerals is gypsum, which is used to make plaster.

Hydroxides

Hydroxide minerals usually form when water reacts with and changes a metallic mineral. Hydroxide minerals contain a hydrogen and oxygen atom joined together (called the hydroxyl radical) in their chemical formula. For example, goethite is formed when water reacts with an iron-rich mineral. In the past, people used goethite as a pigment for cave drawings.

Halides

ROCK SALT

Halides are minerals that are made from a metallic element combined with either the element fluorine, chlorine, iodine, or bromine. One halide that most people are familiar with is halite—which is used to make table salt.

Sulfides

GALENA

Sulfides are minerals that are formed when the element sulfur combines with a metal or semimetal. Galena is an example of a sulfide that's formed when sulfur combines with the metal lead and is used as a lead ore.

Borates

Borate minerals contain a chemical compound called the borate radical, which is made from the elements boron and oxygen. These minerals tend to be soft and are often found in desert areas. One of the most common forms of borate is a mineral called borax, which is used in some laundry detergents.

BORAX

Sulfosalts

When one or more metals combine with sulfur and semimetals, they form sulfosalts. Sulfosalts are mostly rare, and some, such as bournonite, are found near other sulfide minerals.

BOURNONITE

GOLD

CHEMICAL FORMULA **Au**
- COLOR **rich yellow**
- HARDNESS **2.5–3**
- CLEAVAGE **none**
- FRACTURE **jagged**
- STREAK **golden yellow**
- LUSTER **metallic**

Some scientists estimate that there are about 1.6 quadrillion tons of gold deep inside Earth! Unfortunately, only a tiny fraction of this native element makes it to Earth's surface, where it's often found in the veins, or fractures, of quartz, igneous rocks, and sedimentary deposits. It's one of the heaviest minerals, so it collects at the bottom of streams, where prospectors can find it by panning. In the United States, panning for gold started the famous gold rush of 1849. Gold is a precious metal—it does not corrode like other metals and is very valuable. It was one of the world's first forms of money. Entire civilizations have risen and fallen based on humans' quest for gold.

EXPERT'S CIRCLE

FOOL'S GOLD
Thanks to its yellow color and metallic luster, pyrite is often called "fool's gold" because some people have been fooled into believing that it's gold. Unlike gold, pyrite is brittle and will shatter if it's struck with a hammer.

BRIGHT YELLOW COLOR

METALLIC LUSTER

10s spotters

be a ROCK HOUND!
Gold can be hammered into very thin sheets. It is soft and easy to bend into rings, earrings, and bracelets, so jewelers love it! Gold is also shaped into coins, chalices, and even fillings for teeth.

SILVER

CHEMICAL FORMULA Ag
- **COLOR** silver-white; tarnishes dark gray or black when exposed to oxygen
- **HARDNESS** 2.5–3 • **CLEAVAGE** none
- **FRACTURE** jagged • **STREAK** silver-white
- **LUSTER** metallic

The chemical symbol for silver is Ag. It comes from the Latin word *argentum*, which means "white and shining." The description is a fitting one for this brilliant metallic element. Like gold and other precious metals, silver occurs deep inside Earth, but is pushed toward Earth's surface by intense heat and pressure. Most silver is found in volcanic rocks and can occur with minerals such as copper and chalcocite.

EXPOSURE TO OXYGEN CAUSES TARNISH OF GRAY OR BLACK.

10s spotters

SILVER-WHITE COLOR

→ **LOOK FOR THIS** Galena is a lead-bearing mineral with a light gray color, which causes some people to confuse galena with silver. However, silver is whiter and galena is much heavier.

DIG THiS!

Be a gold miner! Just grab a metal pie tin or other shallow pan, find a low stream, and put on a pair of rubber boots. Near the bank, scoop up about a cup of water that contains sand and gravel sediment. Swish around the water and let the lighter bits of sediment wash out of the pan. Since gold is heavier than other particles, it will sink to the bottom of the pan and collect there. Some of the best places to look for gold are downstream of exposed igneous rocks.

COPPER

METALLIC LUSTER

CHEMICAL FORMULA Cu
- COLOR copper-red • HARDNESS 2.5–3 • CLEAVAGE none
- FRACTURE jagged • STREAK copper red • LUSTER metallic

Copper is believed to be one of the first
metals used by humans. Evidence shows
that it was used in tools and ornaments as
early as 8000 B.C.E. In its native form, copper
occurs in fine-grained volcanic rocks called
basalt. Copper also occurs with chalcopyrite and other
minerals as an ore—a solid substance, from which minerals can be extracted. Copper is an excellent conductor of
electricity and is used to make wires.

COPPER-RED COLOR
(WHEN EXPOSED TO
OXYGEN, TURNS GREEN
OR BLACK OVER TIME)

→ **LOOK FOR THIS** Native copper is usually found in
irregular masses, often with strange shapes. Sometimes
it forms branching crystals, called dendrites, which
makes it look like a plant.

SULFUR

CHEMICAL FORMULA S
- COLOR yellow, greenish or reddish yellow, brown, gray
- HARDNESS 1.5–2.5 • CLEAVAGE poor, 2 directions
- FRACTURE irregular, uneven • STREAK white
- LUSTER greasy or resinous • OTHER distinctive odor

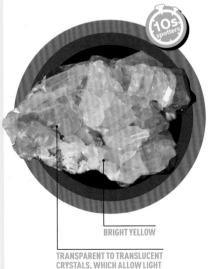

BRIGHT YELLOW

TRANSPARENT TO TRANSLUCENT
CRYSTALS, WHICH ALLOW LIGHT
TO PASS THROUGH

Sulfur is one of the most abundant
elements in the universe and is easily
recognizable thanks to its crystals,
which are usually bright yellow. This
mineral is generally deposited by
volcanic gases in openings near
volcanoes. It often occurs in basalt,
a type of igneous rock. One of the
most distinctive properties of sulfur
is that it smells like rotten eggs!

DIAMOND

GREASY, BRILLIANT LUSTER

CHEMICAL FORMULA C
- COLOR colorless to shades of yellow, red, orange, pink, blue, green, brown, black • HARDNESS 10 • CLEAVAGE perfect, 4 directions • FRACTURE irregular, uneven • STREAK none • LUSTER greasy, brilliant • OTHER transparent to translucent; some are fluorescent

Measuring a whopping 10 on the Mohs Hardness Scale, diamond is the hardest known mineral on Earth. Its strength comes from its composition—carbon atoms packed together by strong chemical bonds. Many people falsely believe that diamonds form from coal, but they actually develop in an igneous rock called peridotite.

SO HARD, IT CAN SCRATCH ANY SOFTER MINERAL

be a ROCK HOUND!

In 1905, a mine superintendent in South Africa discovered a diamond that weighed 1.37 pounds (621 g). That's as heavy as four baseballs!

GRAPHITE

CHEMICAL FORMULA C
- COLOR steel gray to iron black • HARDNESS 1–2
- CLEAVAGE perfect, 1 direction; breaks into thin flakes
- FRACTURE uneven • STREAK grayish to black • LUSTER metallic

Graphite is a mineral found in several types of metamorphic rocks. Its name comes from the Greek word *graphein,* which means "to write." So, it should be no surprise to learn that this mineral is a key ingredient in pencils. Like diamonds, graphite is made of carbon. However, some of the chemical bonds that link its atoms together are weak. This makes graphite significantly softer than diamond.

SO SOFT IT FEELS GREASY WHEN YOU RUB IT BETWEEN YOUR FINGERS

→ **LOOK FOR THIS** In the 1500s, farmers in Cumbria, England, were aware of graphite's ability to leave a mark against almost any surface. They often used the mineral to mark their sheep.

A SIX-SIDED FIGURE

CHEMICAL FORMULA SiO_2
- COLOR clear, white, gray, purple, yellow, brown, black, pink, green, red
- HARDNESS 7 • CLEAVAGE none
- FRACTURE smooth and rounded, like a scallop shell • STREAK white
- LUSTER glassy • OTHER crystals are often long, six-sided prisms and can be transparent like glass

Quartz is a hard mineral that's present in many types of igneous, sedimentary, and metamorphic rocks. It is one of the most common minerals found on continental rocks, and it comes in many different forms. You've likely seen bits of quartz in sand on the beach. However, sandcastle material isn't its only use. Native Americans used flint, a type of quartz, as cutting tools and arrowheads. It was also used in firearms in the 17th and 18th centuries. Today, quartz is used in industrial products, such as glass, ceramics, and cement.

STRIKING PURPLE COLOR

GLASSY LUSTER

PYRAMID-SHAPED CRYSTALS

AMETHYST

Amethyst is a purple variety of quartz. Its color comes from small amounts of iron and manganese in the mineral. Amethyst usually forms short, pointed crystals that look like pyramids and is commonly found inside of geodes. Like tiger's eye, many people use amethyst in jewelry, and it is the birthstone for the month of February. Amethyst is one of the least expensive gemstones.

⚠ DANGER!

Even though quartz is usually harmless—unless its crystals are broken—broken crystals often have razor-sharp edges, which can cause painful cuts. So, handle with care!

ROSE QUARTZ

PINK COLOR

Thanks to its rosy pink color, rose quartz is one of the most sought after forms of quartz. It is fairly common and is found all over the world. Most often rose quartz is used as an inexpensive gemstone after being tumbled and polished. Its crystals have a hazy quality, which makes rose quartz less transparent, but more translucent (allowing light to pass through) than other kinds of quartz.

HAZY, TRANSLUCENT QUALITY

SMOKY QUARTZ

Smoky quartz occurs in a variety of dark shades, including smoky gray, brown, and black. Its color is partly caused by the presence of aluminum. This mineral is commonly found in the U.S. states of New Hampshire and Colorado.

ALWAYS TRANSLUCENT, ALLOWING LIGHT TO PASS THROUGH

CITRINE

Citrine is a light yellowish orange quartz. Its name comes from its citrus-like color, which is likely the result of iron in the crystal structure. As a gemstone, citrine is often confused with topaz, though topaz is harder and heavier.

LIGHT YELLOWISH BROWN

SOMEWHAT TRANSPARENT

PYRAMID-SHAPED CRYSTALS

BROWN AND YELLOW STRIPES

TIGER'S EYE

Tiger's eye is a member of the quartz group that's produced when silica-rich groundwater seeps into and replaces a mineral called crocidolite. Tiger's eye is brown and has a reflective quality, so it's often cut and polished for jewelry.

APPEARS TO TWINKLE IN THE LIGHT

LOOKS LIKE IT'S MADE OF FIBERS

CHALCEDONY

CHEMICAL FORMULA SiO$_2$
- COLOR white, gray, brown, blue, black • HARDNESS 7
- CLEAVAGE none • FRACTURE smooth and rounded, like a scallop shell, or uneven • STREAK white • LUSTER waxy, glassy, or dull • OTHER sometimes weakly fluorescent

Chalcedony is a form of quartz with crystals so small they can't be seen without a microscope. In its pure form, chalcedony is white. But the presence of small amounts of other minerals often causes chalcedony to occur in a wide range of colors. It usually forms in cracks and holes in other rocks, deposited by water that has dissolved silica in it.

PURE CHALCEDONY IS WHITE, HARD, AND FORMS CRUSTS ON OTHER ROCKS.

ONYX

USUALLY BLACK AND WHITE BANDS

Onyx, a type of chalcedony, may be all black or have bands of alternating colors, which are most commonly black and white. These bands are straight and parallel to each other. Onyx is commonly used to make jewelry. Many cameos are carved from onyx.

CARNELIAN

Carnelian is red-orange chalcedony that gets its distinct color from iron oxide. Carnelian was used by ancient Greeks and Romans to make rings and seals.

NORMALLY REDDISH AND TRANSLUCENT

CHRYSOPRASE

MINT GREEN

Chrysoprase is a type of chalcedony with a greenish color that comes from the presence of nickel. This mineral is often used as a gemstone in pendants and rings.

GLASSY LUSTER

JASPER

CHEMICAL FORMULA SiO$_2$
- COLOR red, yellow, brown
- HARDNESS 6–7 ○ CLEAVAGE none
- FRACTURE rounded, like a scallop shell ○ STREAK white
- LUSTER glassy

Jasper is a fine-grained quartz that forms when waters rich in silicon and oxygen trickle into rocks and leave behind deposits. Jasper is usually found combined with other materials—some of which give it a distinct color. For example, hematite causes jasper to appear red, while clay minerals produce a yellowish white or gray color.

10s spotters

OPAQUE (WON'T ALLOW LIGHT TO PASS THROUGH)

OFTEN HAS SMALL VEINS OF WHITE QUARTZ RUNNING THROUGH IT

EXPERT'S CIRCLE

POPPY JASPER

Some forms of jasper have spheres called orbs. The poppy jasper, which can be found in Morgan Hill, California, is one such example. Its orbs come in colors such as red, yellow, and orange. Experts who have studied the orbs believe the shapes may have formed from iron-rich clay that was included with the silica.

be a ROCK HOUND!

The ancient Egyptians sometimes used jasper to make amulets for the dead (at top). The Egyptians believed these ornaments would protect the dead from anyone who would want to harm them in the afterlife.

AGATE

CHEMICAL FORMULA SiO₂
- COLOR bands of white, yellow, gray, pale blue, brown, pink, red, or black • HARDNESS 7
- CLEAVAGE none • FRACTURE rounded, like a scallop shell • STREAK white • LUSTER glassy to waxy

Agate is a type of chalcedony that forms when groundwater that's rich in silica (silicon and oxygen) is deposited in layers in the cavities of volcanic rock. The layers follow the shape of the cavity, which is why they're usually circular, but they can form other patterns, too. Each layer may be a different color, such as white, brown, gray, yellow, pale blue, red, pink, or black. The colors are caused by different materials that get into the groundwater as it's seeping into the cavity.

COLORFUL BANDS, WHICH ARE USUALLY CIRCULAR

10s spotters

EXPERT'S CIRCLE

MOSS AGATE

Moss agate is a form of chalcedony that forms with the mineral hornblende, which gives the agate a greenish color. Despite its name, moss agate is not a true agate because it does not have the mineral's defining feature—the layers of color banding.

COMMONLY FOUND INSIDE GEODES AND IS NOT VISIBLE UNLESS THE GEODE IS CUT

be a ROCK HOUND!

The ancient Egyptians believed that agate was a cure for scorpion poison!

OPAL

CHEMICAL FORMULA $SiO_2 \cdot nH_2O$
- COLOR white, green, black, brown, yellow, gray • HARDNESS 5–6 • CLEAVAGE none
- FRACTURE uneven; brittle; rounded, like a scallop shell • STREAK white
- LUSTER glassy, pearly

Opal is a type of quartz that includes a small amount of water, which is trapped in it as its crystals form. Opal is formed as silica fills in small spaces and can be found in most types of rock. In its pure form, opal is colorless, but the most popular varieties come in shimmery colors that seem to change in the light. The word "opalescent," which means "showing varying colors," is derived from opal.

APPEARS TO SHIMMER IN THE LIGHT

10s spotters

ROUNDED FRACTURE THAT LOOKS LIKE A SCALLOP SHELL

FIRE OPAL
Fire opal, which is most commonly found in Mexico, is a type of opal that's distinguished by its red, yellow, or orange color. Unlike other forms of opal, fire opal is usually transparent or translucent, and it does not shimmer in the light. The warm colors are thought to come from the presence of a small amount of iron oxide.

EXPERT'S CIRCLE

Laugh Out Loud!

Joke: What did the mineral collector say to the rock?

Answer: May the quartz be with you!

PLAGIOCLASE FELDSPAR

CHEMICAL FORMULA $NaAlSi_3O_8$ to $CaAl_2Si_2O_8$
• COLOR white, colorless, gray, green, bluish, reddish • HARDNESS 6 • CLEAVAGE good; 2 cleavage planes that intersect at right angles
• FRACTURE uneven and brittle • STREAK white
• LUSTER glassy; pearly on cleavage
• OTHER transparent to translucent

The plagioclase feldspars form a group of minerals that are commonly found in both igneous and metamorphic rocks. All plagioclase feldspars have the same basic chemical formula, except they vary in the amount of sodium or calcium. Since their composition is similar, so is their structure: All have two cleavage planes that intersect at right angles. Plagioclase feldspars almost always have thin lines, or striations, running across their broken faces—the result of crystals that have grown as twins.

CLEAVAGE SURFACE WITH TINY GROOVES CALLED STRIATIONS

CLEAVAGE PLANES INTERSECTING AT 90-DEGREE ANGLES

NAME GAME

The word "plagioclase" comes from two Greek words: *plagios*, which means "oblique," and *klasis*, which means "to break." The terms refer to the mineral's cleavage.

USUALLY WHITE

HAS TWO CLEAVAGE PLANES AT RIGHT ANGLES

ALBITE

Albite is a sodium-rich member of the plagioclase feldspar group. Its chemical formula is $NaAlSi_3O_8$. Sometimes albite occurs with microcline, a member of the potassium feldspar group. Albite often forms twinned crystals that are tablet shaped. It is typically white, and when ground up, it's used in ceramics. Albite's name comes from the Latin word *albus*, which means "white."

ANDESINE

Andesine is a sodium-rich member of the plagioclase feldspar group and gets its name from a type of lava in the Andes Mountains. It occurs in igneous rocks, such as diorite and andesite, as well as some metamorphic and sedimentary rocks. Andesine typically has very small crystals that can often be "twinned," meaning that the crystals grow in pairs. Its chemical formula is $(Na,Ca)[Al(Si,Al)Si_2O_8]$.

IF VISIBLE, ITS CRYSTALS OFTEN FORM TWINS AND HAVE A PEARLY LUSTER.

CAN BE WHITE, GRAY, OR COLORLESS

LABRADORITE

GLASSY LUSTER

USUALLY DARK BLUE OR GRAY IRIDESCENT COLORS

Labradorite is a calcium-rich member of the plagioclase feldspar group. This mineral is easy to recognize, thanks to its beautiful color, which seems to change when seen from different angles. This effect, called iridescence, is caused by light striking the layers within the mineral's crystal structure. It is named after Labrador, a region in Newfoundland, Canada. Its chemical formula is $(Ca,Na)[Al(Al,Si)Si_2O_8]$.

ANORTHITE

Anorthite is a calcium-rich member of the plagioclase feldspar group. This mineral is usually present in igneous rocks that are abundant in magnesium and iron. Anorthite has also been found in meteorites—debris from comets or asteroids that has landed on Earth. Its chemical formula is $CaAl_2Si_2O_8$.

HAS A GLASSY LUSTER

FORMS SMALL CRYSTALS THAT ARE SHAPED LIKE PRISMS

MICROCLINE

CHEMICAL FORMULA $KAlSi_3O_8$
- COLOR colorless, white, cream to pale yellow, salmon pink to red, bright green to blue-green • HARDNESS 6–6.5
- CLEAVAGE perfect, 2 directions • FRACTURE uneven to rounded, like a scallop shell
- STREAK white • LUSTER glassy, dull

Microcline is a potassium-rich feldspar that's often used in ceramics. It is one of the most common feldspars. It can be found in metamorphic rocks, including gneiss and schist, as well as in igneous rocks like granite and syenite that solidify beneath Earth's surface. Microcline usually forms prismatic crystals that sometimes get quite large.

AMAZONITE

Amazonite is a pretty green type of microcline. Its color may come from small quantities of lead in the mineral. Amazonite is named for the Amazon region of South America, and it can be found in Colorado and Virginia in the United States.

EXPERT'S CIRCLE

SHORT, BLOCKY CRYSTALS THAT ARE OFTEN TWINNED

10S. spotters

WHEN VIEWED WITH A MAGNIFIER, CRYSTALS HAVE A CRISSCROSS PATTERN OF FINE LINES.

DIG THIS!

Although this doesn't hold true for microcline, some minerals are named after places where they can be found. Can you match each mineral below to a place where it is abundant?

Andalusite	Le Baux, France
Florencite	Sharm Abhur, Saudi Arabia
Abhurite	Andalusia, Spain
Bauxite	Melons Mine, California, U.S.A.
Melonite	Florence, Italy

Answers: Andalusite: Andalusia, Spain; Florencite: Florence, Italy; Abhurite: Sharm Abhur, Saudi Arabia; Bauxite: Le Baux, France; Melonite: Melons Mine, California, U.S.A.

ORTHOCLASE

CHEMICAL FORMULA $KAlSi_3O_8$
- COLOR colorless, white, cream, pink, pale yellow, brownish red
- HARDNESS 6–6.5
- CLEAVAGE perfect, 2 directions
- FRACTURE uneven to rounded, like a scallop shell
- STREAK white
- LUSTER glassy

Like microcline, orthoclase is a feldspar that contains potassium. It can be found in metamorphic rocks, such as gneiss, and in igneous rocks that are rich in silica or potassium, especially granite. Crystals formed by orthoclase are usually short and prismatic and can be pink, white, yellow, or red.

10s spotters

SHORT, BLOCKY CRYSTALS

CRYSTAL COLORS CAN VARY AND INCLUDE PINK.

MOONSTONE

Moonstone is a type of orthoclase that appears to glow from the inside. This phenomenon is called the "schiller effect." It is produced when light strikes the inner layers of the mineral and bounces back out.

EXPERT'S CIRCLE

NEPHELINE

CHEMICAL FORMULA (Na,K)AlSiO$_4$
- COLOR colorless, white, gray, reddish, smoky
- HARDNESS 5.5–6 ◦ CLEAVAGE good, 3 directions;
parallel to prism faces ◦ FRACTURE rounded, like a scallop
shell, and brittle ◦ STREAK white ◦ LUSTER greasy, glassy
- OTHER transparent to translucent

Sometimes there just isn't enough silica present in magma or lava for a feldspar to form. In this case, "feldspathoids" are produced. These minerals are similar to feldspars, except they have less silica and have a somewhat different crystal structure. Nepheline is the most common type of feldspathoid and often forms in igneous rocks that are rich in magnesium and iron. Like feldspars, this mineral can be used in ceramics.

GLASSY OR GREASY LUSTER

GOOD, THREE-DIRECTIONAL CLEAVAGE, BUT RARELY FORMS GOOD CRYSTALS

NAME GAME

When nepheline is placed in a strong acid, it becomes clouded. This characteristic inspired the mineral's name, which comes from *nephele*, the Greek word for "cloud."

SODALITE

CHEMICAL FORMULA Na$_8$(Al$_6$Si$_6$O$_{24}$)Cl$_2$
- COLOR blue, gray, white ◦ HARDNESS 5.5–6 ◦ CLEAVAGE poor,
6 directions ◦ FRACTURE uneven to rounded, like a scallop
shell ◦ STREAK white ◦ LUSTER greasy, glassy ◦ OTHER
transparent to translucent

Sodalite, which is named for its high sodium content, is another type of feldspathoid that's found in igneous rock. The mineral is well known for its intense blue color—a characteristic that causes some people to mistake it for the equally blue lapis lazuli. However, a simple streak test can be used to tell the two minerals apart: Sodalite has a white streak, while lapis lazuli has a blue streak.

INTENSE BLUE COLOR

GLASSY OR GREASY LUSTER

LAZURITE

CHEMICAL FORMULA $(Na,Ca)_8(Al,Si)_{12}O_{24}(S,SO)_4$
- **COLOR** blue, violet blue, greenish blue
- **HARDNESS** 5–5.5 • **CLEAVAGE** poor, 6 directions • **FRACTURE** uneven, brittle
- **STREAK** blue • **LUSTER** dull to greasy

You're probably familiar with lapis lazuli, a deep blue gemstone that is often used in jewelry. This gemstone gets its vivid color from lazurite, a mineral that usually forms when carbonate rocks such as limestone are chemically altered. The mineral made news in the 1990s, when large amounts of lazurite crystals were discovered in mines in northern Afghanistan. This occurrence was unusual, because the mineral rarely forms crystals that are visible to the naked eye.

10s. spotters

BRIGHT BLUE

CAN HAVE A GREASY LUSTER

OFTEN FOUND WITH THE MINERAL PYRITE

LAPIS LAZULI

Although lazurite is the main ingredient in lapis lazuli, this gemstone also consists of other minerals, such as pyrite and calcite. Because of its pretty blue color, people have been using lapis lazuli in jewelry and other decorative items for thousands of years.

EXPERT'S CIRCLE

be a ROCK HOUND!

The ancient Egyptians used a powdered form of lazurite as eye shadow.

LEUCITE

CHEMICAL FORMULA $KAlSi_2O_6$
- COLOR colorless, white, gray
- HARDNESS 5.5–6 • CLEAVAGE none or very poor
- FRACTURE smooth and rounded, like a scallop shell
- STREAK white • LUSTER glassy, but changes to dull in older samples

Like nephelite and other feldspathoids, leucite is a mineral that will develop only when there isn't much silica present. It's typically found in fine-grained volcanic rocks such as basalt, but can form crystals that measure up to one inch (2.54 cm) in other igneous rocks. Leucite is usually white, but can be gray as well.

ITS LUSTER CAN BE GLASSY OR DULL.

ITS CRYSTALS ARE USUALLY MASSIVE.

WHEN IT DOES FORM CRYSTALS, THEY LOOK LIKE TRAPEZOIDS.

NATROLITE

CHEMICAL FORMULA $Na_2Al_2Si_3O_{10} \cdot 2H_2O$
- COLOR white, colorless, pale pink, red, yellow, green, gray • HARDNESS 5.5–5 • CLEAVAGE perfect, 1 direction
- FRACTURE uneven, brittle • STREAK colorless to white
- LUSTER glassy, silky • OTHER crystals are transparent to translucent

Thanks to its long, needlelike crystals, which can grow up to a whopping three feet (1 m), natrolite is an easy mineral to spot. Natrolite generally is found in spaces that form in volcanic igneous rocks, such as basalt. It also creates veins in granite and in metamorphic rocks, such as gneiss.

USUALLY HAS LONG, SLENDER CRYSTALS THAT ARE TRANSPARENT OR TRANSLUCENT

be a ROCK HOUND!

Natrolite is one of the few minerals that produces an electric charge when it's put under pressure.

HEULANDITE

CHEMICAL FORMULA $(CaAl_2Si_7O_{18}) \cdot 6H_2O$
- COLOR white, colorless, gray, red, greenish
- HARDNESS 3.5–4 • CLEAVAGE perfect,
1 direction • FRACTURE uneven, brittle
- STREAK colorless to white • LUSTER pearly,
glassy • OTHER crystals are transparent
to translucent

Heulandites belong to a family of minerals called zeolites, which are most often found filling cavities in igneous rocks, such as basalt. Heulandites are usually white or colorless. Sometimes they form visible crystals that are long and wide at the center. This gives them a coffinlike appearance!

CRYSTALS ARE COFFIN-SHAPED.

PEARLY OR GLASSY LUSTER

MESOLITE

CHEMICAL FORMULA $Na_2Ca_2(Al_6Si_9)O_{30} \cdot 8H_2O$
- COLOR white, colorless • HARDNESS 5 • CLEAVAGE perfect,
2 directions • FRACTURE uneven • STREAK colorless to white
- LUSTER silky, glassy • OTHER crystals are transparent to
translucent

Mesolite is a mineral that forms masses of long, needlelike crystals that can resemble hair. Because of its appearance, it is often confused with natrolite. However, it is softer and less dense than natrolite. Mesolite usually occurs in the cavities of igneous rocks, such as basalt and andesite. It can also be found in veins in other igneous rocks.

SILKY, NEEDLELIKE CRYSTALS

be a ROCK HOUND!

Sometimes mesolite forms tufts or hairlike crystals. When this happens, it's called "cotton stone."

CHABAZITE

CHEMICAL FORMULA CaAl$_2$Si$_4$O$_{12}$ • 6H$_2$O
- COLOR white, yellow, pink, red ○ HARDNESS : 4–5
- CLEAVAGE poor, 3 directions ○ FRACTURE uneven, brittle ○ STREAK white ○ LUSTER glassy
- OTHER crystals are transparent to translucent

MANY CRYSTALS MAY APPEAR AS TWINS.

Chabazite is in the zeolite family and can be found filling openings in volcanic igneous rocks, such as basalt. It's also been seen as veins in granite and pegmatites and in some metamorphic rocks. It often forms crystals called rhombs, which are shaped like bent cubes. Its crystal structure allows it to be used as a natural filter, removing certain chemicals from gases.

CRYSTALS SHAPED LIKE BENT CUBES

be a ROCK HOUND!

Chabazite powder added to pig feed can help reduce stinky odors from the ammonium in pig waste.

ANALCIME

CHEMICAL FORMULA NaAlSi$_2$O$_6$ • H$_2$O
- COLOR white, colorless, gray with greenish, yellowish, or reddish tints ○ HARDNESS 5.5–5 ○ CLEAVAGE none
- FRACTURE uneven to somewhat rounded ○ STREAK colorless
- LUSTER glassy, silky ○ OTHER crystals are transparent to translucent

Analcime is a mineral in the zeolite family that forms in the cavities of igneous rocks, such as basalt and granite, and in metamorphic rocks, such as gneiss. It also occurs as a sedimentary deposit in areas once covered by salty lakes. The mineral's name comes from the Greek word *analkimos*, which means "weak." The word refers to the mineral's tendency to produce a weak static electric charge when heated or rubbed.

SHINY, CLEAR, TRAPEZOID-SHAPED CRYSTALS LINE ROCK CAVITIES.

be a ROCK HOUND!

Analcime is often used as an ingredient in cement or concrete.

APOPHYLLITE

CHEMICAL FORMULA $KCa_4Si_8O_{20}(F,OH) \cdot 8H_2O$ • COLOR colorless, white, pale pink, pale to emerald green • HARDNESS 4.5–5 • CLEAVAGE perfect, 1 direction • FRACTURE uneven • STREAK white • LUSTER glassy, pearly • OTHER transparent to translucent

Apophyllite is a type of silicate mineral that's usually found in basalt with members of the zeolite family. It also occurs in metamorphic rocks. Apophyllite is known for its striking crystals that can measure up to eight inches (20 cm) across. The crystals either form cubes or pyramids and come in an assortment of colors, but clear and green are the most prized by collectors.

FORMS CUBIC OR PYRAMID-LIKE CRYSTALS

NAME GAME

The name "apophyllite" comes from the Greek words *apo* and *phyllazein*, which mean "to get" and "leaf." The name is inspired by apophyllite's tendency to separate into layers or flakes when heated.

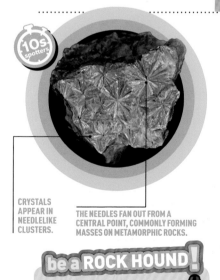

CRYSTALS APPEAR IN NEEDLELIKE CLUSTERS.

THE NEEDLES FAN OUT FROM A CENTRAL POINT, COMMONLY FORMING MASSES ON METAMORPHIC ROCKS.

be a ROCK HOUND!

Powdered pyrophyllite is often added to lipstick to make It shine.

PYROPHYLLITE

CHEMICAL FORMULA $Al_2Si_4O_{10}(OH)_2$ • COLOR colorless, white, cream, brownish green, pale blue, or gray • HARDNESS 1–2 • CLEAVAGE perfect, 1 direction • FRACTURE uneven, splintery • STREAK white • LUSTER pearly to dull • OTHER translucent to opaque

Pyrophyllite is a soft mineral that often occurs in metamorphic rocks such as schist with minerals such as quartz, albite, and andalusite. Pyrophyllite doesn't always form crystals, but when they do occur, the crystals look like needlelike clusters that radiate, or fan out, from a central point.

TALC

CHEMICAL FORMULA $Mg_3Si_4O_{10}(OH)_2$
- COLOR white, apple green • HARDNESS 1
- CLEAVAGE perfect, 1 direction
- FRACTURE uneven • STREAK white
- LUSTER greasy • OTHER translucent to opaque

Talc is a very soft mineral that's found in metamorphic rocks, such as schists and marbles. It is used in many plastics, paints, and ceramics, but you're probably most familiar with it in its finely ground-up form—talcum powder. Since talcum powder has the ability to absorb moisture and odors, it is a key ingredient in body and foot powders. Talc is also used as a dry lubricant to keep machinery parts moving smoothly.

SOAPSTONE

Soapstone is a metamorphic rock made mainly of talc. This quality makes soapstone an easy rock to carve. Nearly 5,000 years ago, Native Americans in eastern North America carved soapstone into cooking bowls. Because it heats evenly, soapstone is often used around fireplaces and wood stoves. Large deposits of soapstone have been found in the U.S. states of New York, Vermont, and Connecticut.

EXPERT'S CIRCLE

GREASY LUSTER

WHITE OR GREENISH COLOR

10s spotters

⚠️ ☠️ **DANGER!**
Since talcum powder is fine-grained, be careful to not inhale it. It may cause severe respiratory problems.

MUSCOVITE

CHEMICAL FORMULA $KAl_2(Si_3Al)O_{10}(OH)_2$
• COLOR colorless, white, yellowish, greenish, pink, brownish, multicolored
• HARDNESS 2–2.5 • CLEAVAGE perfect, 1 direction • FRACTURE uneven
• STREAK colorless • LUSTER glassy, pearly • OTHER translucent to transparent

Muscovite belongs to a group of silicate minerals called mica, which cleave, or split, into thin, elastic sheets. Muscovite can be found in many environments, but typically occurs in a metamorphic rock called schist and a type of igneous rock called pegmatite.

PERFECT CLEAVAGE FORMS THIN, ELASTIC SHEETS OR FLAKES.

10S spotters

SELENITE GYPSUM

Muscovite is sometimes confused with another mineral called selenite gypsum. Like muscovite, selenite gypsum can have transparent crystals and a single, perfect cleavage. But unlike muscovite, selenite gypsum does not split into thin, elastic sheets.

EXPERT'S CIRCLE

NAME GAME

The name "muscovite" comes from Muscovy, a region in Russia where the mineral was once used to make window glass.

BIOTITE

CHEMICAL FORMULA $K(Mg,Fe)_{3}(AlFe)Si_3O_{10}(OH,F)_2$
COLOR black, brownish black, greenish black, dark green
- HARDNESS 2.5–3 • CLEAVAGE perfect, 1 direction
- FRACTURE uneven • STREAK colorless • LUSTER glassy, pearly

Biotite is the name given to a group of usually deep brown or black mica minerals frequently found in igneous and metamorphic rocks. These include granite, pegmatite, gneiss, and schist.

Biotite crystals are usually tabular—shaped like a pad of paper. All biotite minerals have perfect cleavage that forms thin, flexible sheets that can break if bent severely. Most biotite is found as small, dark-colored grains embedded in the rock. Geologists use biotite in their research—sometimes for analyzing the temperature histories of metamorphic rocks. At other times, they use it for determining the approximate ages of igneous rocks. Yellowish-tinted biotite can look like pyrite.

PHLOGOPITE

Phlogopite is a magnesium-rich member of the biotite group, whereas other members may be high in iron. Phlogopite is a poor conductor of electricity and is often used as an insulator in electrical components.

EXPERT'S CIRCLE

BLACK OR DARK BROWN

10s spotters

FLAKY CLEAVAGE

be a ROCK HOUND!

To determine how old igneous rocks are, scientists use a type of radioactive age-dating technique.

GLAUCONITE

DULL LUSTER

OFTEN BLUE-GREEN

CHEMICAL FORMULA $(K,Na)(Mg,Al,Fe)_2(Si,Al)_4O_{10}(OH,F)_2$
COLOR blue-green, yellow-green, green • HARDNESS 2 • CLEAVAGE perfect
• FRACTURE uneven • STREAK green • LUSTER dull

Glauconite is a mica mineral named after the Greek word *glaukos*, which means "blue-green." The term refers to the mineral's color. Glauconite forms in shallow marine environments ranging from 100 to 3,000 feet (30 to 1,000 m) below sea level. It can often be found in marine sediments known as greensand and in clay and sand formations. It is often made up of rounded pellets of fine-grained particles and may contain fragments of shells—and even fossils. Scientists have found that some pellets come from animal-made materials, including poop!

be a ROCK HOUND!

Glauconite has been used as a pigment in green oil paints for centuries. These paints were especially popular during the Middle Ages, when they were used by Russian artists to create religious paintings.

VERMICULITE

LAYERING EFFECT

CLEAVAGE FORMS THIN, ELASTIC SHEETS.

CHEMICAL FORMULA $(Mg,Fe,Al)_3(Al,Si)_4O_{10}(OH) \cdot 4H_2O$ COLOR colorless, green, grayish white, yellowish brown • HARDNESS 1–2 • CLEAVAGE perfect
• FRACTURE uneven • STREAK white • LUSTER oily, earthy

Vermiculite is a group of mica minerals. The first major deposit was found in Colorado, U.S.A, in 1913. Vermiculite can often be found as green, brown, or golden yellow particles in soil and in some igneous rocks. Like other mica minerals, vermiculite has cleavage that forms thin, elastic sheets. When vermiculite minerals are heated to a temperature above 1598°F (870°C), they can expand to 20 times their original thickness!

NAME GAME

Vermiculite's ability to expand quickly inspired the group's name. It comes from the Latin word *vermiculus*, which means "little worm." Many gardeners use vermiculite like worms—to aerate their soil. You may have some in your garden or in a flower pot in your house!

LEPIDOLITE

10s spotters

CHEMICAL FORMULA $K(Li,Al_3)(Al,Si_3)O_{10}(OH,F)_2$
- COLOR violet, pale yellow, grayish white
- HARDNESS 2.5-3 • CLEAVAGE perfect • FRACTURE uneven
- STREAK colorless • LUSTER pearly

Lepidolite is a type of mica mineral that contains lithium—an element used to make glass and enamels. The mineral rarely forms well-developed crystals, but when it does, they are usually hexagonal, or six-sided, and can measure one to two inches (2.5 to 5 cm) long. Lepidolite is often pale lilac and can be found in granitic pegmatite. It occurs with other minerals, such as tourmaline and quartz.

CAN HAVE HEXAGONAL CRYSTALS

IS OFTEN LILAC-COLORED

PEARLY LUSTER

CHRYSOCOLLA

10s spotters

CHEMICAL FORMULA $Cu_2H_2(Si_2O_5)(OH)_4 \cdot nH_2O$
- COLOR blue, blue-green, green • HARDNESS 2-4
- CLEAVAGE none • FRACTURE uneven to rounded, like a scallop shell • STREAK pale blue, tan, gray
- LUSTER glassy, earthy

OFTEN BLUE

ITS CRYSTALS ARE RARELY VISIBLE.

Chrysocolla is often found in copper deposits along with quartz, chalcedony, and opal. Chrysocolla is usually sky blue, and as a result can be confused with another blue mineral—turquoise. However, a simple hardness test will show that chrysocolla is a much softer mineral.

be a ROCK HOUND!

Roman emperor Nero was a huge fan of the "Greens," a chariot-racing team. Before big competitions, he would have the stadium sand sprinkled with green chrysocolla to show his support.

BENTONITE

CHEMICAL FORMULA
$(NaCa_{0.5})_{0.33}(Al,Mg)_2Si_4O_{10}(OH)_2 \cdot nH_2O$
- COLOR yellow, white, gray • HARDNESS 1–2
- CLEAVAGE perfect, 2 directions • FRACTURE uneven
- STREAK white to buff • LUSTER earthy

VERY SOFT

The word "bentonite" is used to describe a group of earthy clay minerals that are usually considered to be secondary minerals because they form from volcanic ash that has been changed over time by water. There are three types of bentonite minerals; each one is named after its dominant element: potassium bentonite, sodium bentonite, and calcium bentonite. Bentonite minerals can be yellow, white, or gray and are used in bricks and ceramics.

EARTHY LUSTER

ITS CRYSTALS ARE NOT VISIBLE TO THE HUMAN EYE WITHOUT A MICROSCOPE.

KAOLINITE

CHEMICAL FORMULA $Al_2Si_2O_5(OH)_4$
- COLOR white, gray, yellowish • HARDNESS 2–2.5
- CLEAVAGE perfect, 1 direction • FRACTURE none
- STREAK white • LUSTER earthy

Kaolinite is a clay mineral that often forms when water, dissolved carbon dioxide, and acids react with certain mica and feldspar minerals. Kaolinite is considered an important nonmetallic element because it has so many different uses: It is used in paints, as building material to make bricks, and even as a filler in chocolate!

EARTHY LUSTER

OFTEN FORMS DENSE LAYERS THAT ARE EASILY BROKEN AND CRUSHED WHEN SQUEEZED WITH YOUR HAND

be a ROCK HOUND!

The composition of porcelain remained a mystery in Europe until the early 1700s. Around that time, a French Jesuit missionary in China learned that kaolinite was a key ingredient, and he sent a sample to Paris as proof.

TREMOLITE

CHEMICAL FORMULA $Ca_2(Mg,Fe_2)_5Si_8O_{22}(OH)_2$
- COLOR colorless, white, gray-green to dark green
- HARDNESS 5–6 • CLEAVAGE perfect; 2 directions lengthwise in the shape of a diamond
- FRACTURE splintery, brittle • STREAK colorless to white • LUSTER glassy to silky

Tremolite is a member of a common rock-forming mineral group called amphiboles. It contains calcium, magnesium, and iron and often occurs in metamorphic rocks—often those that result from impure limestone or dolomite. There are many varieties of tremolite that range in texture. Some are soft and feathery, while others are leathery.

MOUNTAIN LEATHER

Tremolite is one of half a dozen minerals that form "mountain leather," which has fibrous, matted crystals and is named for its leatherlike appearance. Mountain leather is very absorbent, so it can soak up water easily. When wet, it looks like wet leather. It's also called "mountain wood" or "mountain paper."

EXPERT'S CIRCLE

PRISMATIC CRYSTALS THAT MAY FORM IN FEATHERY CLUSTERS OR LONG PARALLEL FIBERS

10s. spotters

LUSTER IS GLASSY OR SILKY.

⚠️ DANGER!

Because it's fireproof, fibrous tremolite is often used to make asbestos. In the past, it was frequently used as an insulator around pipes and in buildings and is very dangerous to breathe in because it can cause lung cancer. If you have a sample of fibrous tremolite, you should not pull the fibers apart or hold it near your nose or mouth, and always wash your hands after handling this mineral.

ACTINOLITE

CHEMICAL FORMULA $Ca_2(Mg,Fe)_5Si_8O_{22}(OH)_2$
• COLOR bright to dark green, grayish green, black • HARDNESS 5–6 • CLEAVAGE perfect; 2 directions lengthwise in the shape of a diamond • FRACTURE splintery
• STREAK colorless • LUSTER glassy, pearly, silky

Actinolite is a common rock-forming mineral belonging to the same group as tremolite. It is similar to tremolite in its chemical composition and its long and prismatic crystal structure. Actinolite usually forms as a result of metamorphism and is found in several different types of metamorphic rocks, along with minerals such as chlorite, albite, muscovite, and epidote.

DISTINCTIVE CLEAVAGE PATTERN

10s spotters

THIN, PRISMATIC CRYSTALS THAT OFTEN FORM BLADES

NAME GAME

"Actinolite" comes from the Greek word *aktis*. The word means "ray" and refers to the way the crystals radiate, or fan out, from a central point.

EXPERT'S CIRCLE

NEPHRITE

Nephrite is a type of either tremolite or actinolite that's made of tough, interwoven fibers. Nephrite forms jade, a tough stone that's not only worn as jewelry, but has also been used to make blades since the Stone Age. Another mineral called jadeite also forms jade. The jade that comes from jadeite is more valuable than nephrite jade.

HORNBLENDE

CHEMICAL FORMULA $(Ca,Na,K)_{2-3}(Mg,Fe,Al)_5(SiAl)_8O_{22}(OH)$ • COLOR black, dark brown, green • HARDNESS 5–6 • CLEAVAGE perfect; 2 directions in the shape of a diamond • FRACTURE uneven, splintery • STREAK colorless • LUSTER glassy, pearly, silky

Hornblende is the name given to a variety of rock-forming minerals that are rich in iron and magnesium. These members of the amphibole group are very common, especially in metamorphic rocks, such as gneiss and amphibolite, as well as in igneous rocks, such as granite and diorite. They can be easily distinguished by their wedge-shaped cleavage. Hornblende minerals can be black, dark brown, or green and can be either massive or form large, prismatic crystals.

PYROXENE

Like the amphibole group that includes hornblende, pyroxene is a group of rock-forming silicate minerals. The two groups are often mistaken for each other because they have a similar color and hardness. However, pyroxenes have square-shaped cleavage sections. Hornblende's wedge-shaped cleavage is different.

PRISMATIC CRYSTALS

DARK COLOR

10s spotters

WEDGE-SHAPED CLEAVAGE

EXPERT'S CIRCLE

NAME GAME

Because of its color and luster, hornblende was often mistaken in the past for a metallic ore, but the mineral did not produce a useful metal. This may explain the name of the mineral, which comes from the two German words *horn*, meaning "the color of horn," and *blenden*, meaning "to deceive."

GLAUCOPHANE

CHEMICAL FORMULA $Na_2(Mg_3Al_2)Si_8O_{22}(OH)_2$
- COLOR blue, lavender-blue, bluish black
- HARDNESS 6 • CLEAVAGE perfect; 2 directions in the shape of a diamond • FRACTURE uneven, splintery, or rounded • STREAK grayish blue
- LUSTER glassy, pearly • OTHER translucent on thin edges

Glaucophone is rich in magnesium like hornblende. It's found in metamorphic rocks such as blue schist. Normally, it occurs with other minerals, such as lawsonite, albite, and almandine, where it is considered to be an indicator of low-temperature/high-pressure metamorphism. Although glaucophane crystals are usually slender prisms, they can also be massive, fibrous, and granular.

BLUISH BLACK COLOR

10s. spotters

CRYSTALS ARE USUALLY PRISMATIC, WITH A DIAMOND-SHAPED CROSS SECTION.

FERROGLAUCOPHANE
Sometimes, iron will replace magnesium in glaucophane's structure. When this happens, a mineral called ferroglaucophane is formed. The mineral is similar to glaucophane, except that it is darker and denser because of the added iron. It changes from violet to blue to colorless, depending on the angle from which you view it.

EXPERT'S CIRCLE

Laugh Out Loud!

Joke: What eating utensil can you make from potassium, nickel, and iron?

Answer: Knife

ROCK STARS: Birthstones

Amethyst
MONTH: February
STANDS FOR: Sincerity

Aquamarine
MONTH: March
STANDS FOR: Courage

Garnet
MONTH: January
STANDS FOR: Loyalty
FAMOUS SETTING: Each of the garnets in the famous pyrope hairpin from the Victorian era is cut in a rose shape.

Diamond
MONTH: April
STANDS FOR: Enduring Love

Birthstones

A birthstone is a gem that represents the month in which a person is born. No one is really sure where the idea of birthstones came from, but one popular belief is that they were inspired by a biblical story that involved a character who wore a type of armor called a breastplate, made of 12 different stones. Today, most people know their birthstone and may wear it in a ring or necklace just for fun. But in the past, some cultures associated a deeper meaning with each stone. Some believed a birthstone represented the wearer's character traits or brought a person luck. Find your birthstone here, and discover the emotion or trait it was believed to represent.

Emerald
MONTH: May
STANDS FOR: Pure Love
FAMOUS SETTING: Legend says the Hooker emerald was once worn in a sultan's belt buckle. Now it's a brooch with 129 diamonds.

Pearl
MONTH: June
STANDS FOR: Enduring Love

Ruby
MONTH: July
STANDS FOR: Contentment

Peridot
MONTH: August
STANDS FOR: Happiness

Opal
MONTH: October
STANDS FOR: Hope

Topaz
MONTH: November
STANDS FOR: Faithfulness

Turquoise
MONTH: December
STANDS FOR: Success

Sapphire
MONTH: September
STANDS FOR: Clear Thinking
FAMOUS SETTING: The Gordon star sapphire ring is surrounded by 24 pear-shaped diamonds.

RIEBECKITE

CHEMICAL FORMULA $Na_2(Fe^{2+}_3 Fe^{3+}_2)Si_8O_{22}(OH)_2$
- COLOR grayish blue to dark blue, black • HARDNESS 5–6
- CLEAVAGE perfect; 2 directions in the shape of a diamond
- FRACTURE uneven, splintery • STREAK white to blue-gray
- LUSTER glassy, silky • OTHER translucent to opaque

Riebeckite is a type of silicate that contains sodium and iron. It often occurs in igneous rocks that are rich in feldspar and quartz, such as granite and rhyolite. Riebeckite is usually grayish blue to dark blue, but can be even darker if more iron is present. The mineral was named in honor of Emil Riebeck, a famous German explorer and mineralogist who lived in the 19th century.

DEEP GRAYISH BLUE COLOR; PRISMATIC CRYSTALS

TINY GROOVES CALLED STRIATIONS MAY ALSO BE PRESENT.

be a ROCK HOUND!

Ailsite is a type of granite found in Scotland that contains large amounts of riebeckite. It is used to make stones for the sport of curling.

VISIBLE CRYSTALS TEND TO BE SHORT PRISMS.

ENSTATITE

CHEMICAL FORMULA $Mg_2Si_2O_6$
- COLOR colorless, pale yellow, pale green, greenish brown, black • HARDNESS 5–6 • CLEAVAGE good to perfect; 2 directions at right angles • FRACTURE uneven • STREAK gray to white
- LUSTER glassy

Enstatite belongs to a group of minerals called pyroxenes, which share the same structure. Enstatite often occurs in igneous rocks that are rich in magnesium and iron. It has also been found in samples taken from meteorites.

NAME GAME

The name "enstatite" comes from the Greek word *enstates*, which means "opponent." Since enstatite has a high melting point, the term refers to the mineral's resistance to heat. A weathered type of enstatite, called bronzite for its bronzelike color and metallic luster, is used as a gemstone.

AUGITE

CHEMICAL FORMULA (Ca,Na)(Mg,Fe,Al,Ti)(Si,Al)$_2$O$_6$
• COLOR bright to dark green, grayish green,
brown, black • HARDNESS 5–6 • CLEAVAGE good;
2 directions lengthwise at almost right angles
• FRACTURE uneven, brittle • STREAK pale brown
to greenish • LUSTER glassy, submetallic, dull

Augite is the most common
member of the pyroxene group
of minerals. It is known for its
dark color and short, thick crystals
that measure up to .5 inches (1.25 cm)
across. Augite can be found in igneous
rocks that don't contain a lot of silica.
This includes diorite, gabbro, basalt, and
andesite. It is also present in some high-
temperature metamorphic rocks.

NAME GAME

The name "augite" comes from the
Greek word *augites,* which means
"brightness." You might think this is
odd considering the mineral's dark
color. However, the word actually
refers to augite's sometimes shiny
appearance.

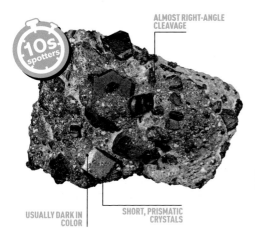

10s spotters

ALMOST RIGHT-ANGLE CLEAVAGE

USUALLY DARK IN COLOR

SHORT, PRISMATIC CRYSTALS

Laugh Out Loud!

Joke: Why is the basalt sad?

Answer: It's always being taken for granite.

DIOPSIDE

CHEMICAL FORMULA $MgCaSi_2O_6$
- COLOR greenish, white, colorless • HARDNESS 5–6
- CLEAVAGE good; 2 directions lengthwise at nearly right angles • FRACTURE uneven • STREAK white to greenish white • LUSTER glassy, dull • OTHER transparent to translucent

Diopside is a pyroxene mineral with prismatic crystals. The crystal faces usually occur in sets of two and are very similar to each other. This characteristic is likely responsible for the mineral's name, which comes from the Greek words for "double" and "appearance." Diopside can often be found in metamorphosed limestone and dolomite and in igneous rocks, such as peridotites and kimberlites.

OFTEN GREEN, BUT CAN ALSO BE WHITE OR COLORLESS

PRISMATIC CRYSTALS

be a ROCK HOUND!

Chrome diopside is a forest-green mineral that's used as a gemstone. The presence of chromium is largely responsible for the mineral's pretty green color.

SPODUMENE

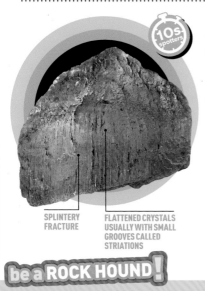

CHEMICAL FORMULA $LiAlSi_2O_6$
- COLOR white, gray, yellowish, emerald green, pink to purple • HARDNESS 6.5–7 • CLEAVAGE good; 2 directions lengthwise at nearly right angles • FRACTURE uneven, splintery • STREAK white • LUSTER glassy, pearly

SPLINTERY FRACTURE

FLATTENED CRYSTALS USUALLY WITH SMALL GROOVES CALLED STRIATIONS

Spodumene is another pyroxene mineral. Its name comes from the Greek word *spudemos*, which means "reduced to ashes." The word refers to the mineral's color, which is usually gray. Spodumene is found only in granite pegmatites and occurs with minerals such as tourmaline, albite, and lepidolite.

be a ROCK HOUND!

A spodumene crystal discovered in South Dakota, U.S.A., measured 47 feet (14.3 m) long. That's longer than a school bus!

JADEITE

CHEMICAL FORMULA $NaAlSi_2O_6$
- COLOR apple green or emerald green to white; lilac, pink, purple, brown, red, yellow
- HARDNESS 6.5–7 • CLEAVAGE distinct; 2 directions at almost right angles
- FRACTURE splintery, uneven
- STREAK white • LUSTER glassy, dull, waxy
- OTHER translucent to opaque

Jadeite is the most common mineral found in jade, a green gemstone used in jewelry. Believe it or not, pure jadeite is actually white. The mineral gets its green color from iron when it's present. Jadeite, usually found in metamorphic rocks, may also appear in other colors, such as lilac, pink, purple, brown, red, and yellow, depending on the elements present.

IDENTIFIED IN THE FIELD BY ITS DISTINCT, NEAR-RIGHT-ANGLE CLEAVAGE

NAME GAME

In the past, people believed that jadeite could cause kidney problems if it was held against the side of the body. The mineral gets its name from the Spanish expression *piedra de ijada*, which means "stone of the side."

EXPERT'S CIRCLE

LILAC JADEITE

Lilac jadeite is a rare form of jadeite that gets its distinctive purple color from the presence of the element manganese. Lilac jadeite is prized because its color is often associated with royalty and sophistication. Like other types of jadeite, this variety can often be found as loose pebbles and rock fragments in stream deposits near the boundaries of tectonic plates that are actively shifting. That's also where you find volcanoes!

BERYL

CHEMICAL FORMULA $Be_3Al_2Si_6O_{18}$
- COLOR bright green, blue, greenish blue, yellow, red, pink, white, colorless • HARDNESS 7.5–8
- CLEAVAGE indistinct, 1 direction
- FRACTURE uneven to rounded, like a scallop shell • STREAK colorless • LUSTER glassy
- OTHER translucent

Beryl is a mineral with a crystal structure that's roomy enough to accommodate atoms from other elements. When this happens, common beryl can be transformed from its usual white or light green color to shades of pink, blue, yellow, and bright green, depending on the element. These colored forms of beryl are often cut and polished into gemstones that you might recognize as emerald, aquamarine, and morganite—to name a few. Beryl is often found in igneous rocks called granite pegmatites. It is also present in some metamorphic rocks, such as schist.

QUARTZ

Because beryl crystals often form hexagonal prisms, beryl can be confused with quartz. But beryl crystals have striations on the surface that run the length of the crystal, whereas quartz crystals have striations that run across the crystal. Beryl is also slightly harder than quartz, so a simple scratch test can tell them apart.

EXPERT'S CIRCLE

10s spotters

SIX-SIDED CRYSTALS, GLASSY LUSTER

COMMON FORM IS WHITE OR LIGHT GREEN.

be a ROCK HOUND!

Beryl has been mined for commercial uses from pegmatite deposits in several U.S. New England states. These same deposits have yielded large quantities of aquamarine and morganite, two of the colored varieties of beryl.

EMERALD

Emerald is a bright green form of beryl that gets its color from chromium and vanadium. This popular gemstone has been mined for thousands of years. Records show that the ancient Egyptians obtained emerald from Upper Egypt as early as 2000 B.C.E. Today, emerald can be found in various regions around the world, but the greatest source comes from Colombia, in South America.

IF VISIBLE, ITS CRYSTALS OFTEN FORM TWINS AND HAVE A PEARLY LUSTER.

CAN BE WHITE, GRAY, OR COLORLESS, ALTHOUGH USUALLY BRIGHT GREEN

AQUAMARINE

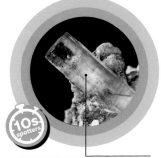

KNOWN FOR GREENISH BLUE COLOR AND CLARITY; HAS SIX-SIDED CRYSTALS LIKE OTHER FORMS OF BERYL

Aquamarine is a greenish blue gemstone that results from the presence of iron in beryl. Aquamarine tends to form crystals that are clearer and larger than those of emerald. One clear crystal that was extracted from a mine in Brazil weighed nearly 243 pounds (110 kg). That's as heavy as a baby elephant!

MORGANITE

Morganite, the least common form of beryl, gets its pink color from the presence of cesium. Although morganite has been around for millions of years, it didn't get an official name until 1911, when it was named after a famous banker and mineral collector—J.P. Morgan. Morganite is found in pegmatites in California and New England in the United States.

PINKISH COLOR

LIKE ALL FORMS OF BERYL, IT HAS SIX-SIDED CRYSTALS.

TOURMALINE

CHEMICAL FORMULA $Na(Mg,Fe)_3Al_6(BO_3)_3(Si_6O_{18})(OH,F)_4$
• COLOR varieties range from black to blue, pink and red, brown, green, multicolored; rarely white • HARDNESS 7-7.5 • CLEAVAGE none • FRACTURE uneven; rounded, like a scallop shell • STREAK colorless to white • LUSTER glassy • OTHER transparent to opaque; brittle

Tourmaline is the name given to a group of 11 silicate minerals that share the same crystal structure, though vary in their chemical makeup. Tourmaline minerals form columnar crystals that often have a triangular cross section. One of the most common forms of tourmaline is schorl, a black, glassy mineral that gets its color from iron. Like all tourmaline, the best-formed schorl crystals are usually found in igneous rocks called pegmatites. Tourmaline can also be found in some types of metamorphic rock.

ELBAITE

Elbaite is a member of the tourmaline group that is gemstone quality. Elbaite can occur in just about any color, and in some cases can exhibit two or three different colors. The mineral is named after Elba, Italy, where it was discovered.

EXPERT'S CIRCLE

HEXAGONAL CRYSTALS HAVE STRIATIONS ALONG THEIR LENGTH.

GLASSY LUSTER

10s spotters

LONG, ROUNDED CRYSTALS, USUALLY WITH A TRIANGULAR CROSS SECTION AND NO CLEAVAGE

be a ROCK HOUND!

When people died during the Victorian era in Great Britain, their relatives often wore schorl jewelry as a symbol of mourning.

HEMIMORPHITE

CHEMICAL FORMULA $Zn_4Si_2O_7(OH)_2 \cdot H_2O$
- **COLOR** white, colorless, yellowish, bluish, brownish
- **HARDNESS** 4.5–5 • **CLEAVAGE** perfect, 1 direction
- **FRACTURE** uneven; rounded, like a scallop shell
- **STREAK** colorless to white • **LUSTER** glassy, brilliant to dull • **OTHER** transparent to translucent; brittle

Hemimorphite is a mineral that gets its name from two Greek words: *hemi*, which means "half," and *morphe*, which means "form." The words refer to the mineral's crystals, which are different at each end. One end is either pointed or rounded, while the other is flat. Hemimorphite is usually colorless or white, but some specimens can appear pale yellow, green, or a vibrant sky blue. Hemimorphite contains zinc and forms as a result of chemical changes in other zinc-rich minerals, such as sphalerite.

CRYSTAL ENDS CAN APPEAR GLOBULAR, MAKING THE CRYSTALS LOOK LIKE A CLUSTER OF GRAPES.

be a ROCK HOUND!

In the past, both hemimorphite and smithsonite were called calamine. Finally, they were given two different names to show that they were two different minerals.

AXINITE

CHEMICAL FORMULA $(Ca,Mn,Fe,Mg)_3Al_2BSi_4O_{15}(OH)$ • **COLOR** clove brown, yellow, violet, greenish, gray, black • **HARDNESS** 6.5–7
• **CLEAVAGE** good, 1 direction • **FRACTURE** uneven; rounded, like a scallop shell • **STREAK** colorless to light brown
• **LUSTER** glassy • **OTHER** transparent to translucent; brittle

Axinite is the name for a group of closely related minerals that all have crystals shaped like the head of an ax. There are four minerals in this group, with ferroaxinite being the most common. Axinites can be found in some low-temperature metamorphic rocks and in igneous rocks that are rich in magnesium and iron.

USUALLY HAS FLATTENED CRYSTALS WITH KNIFELIKE EDGES

OFTEN CLOVE BROWN IN COLOR

be a ROCK HOUND!

Axinite gemstones, which can range from clove brown to violet, are popular with mineral collectors.

EPIDOTE

USUALLY PISTACHIO GREEN

CHEMICAL FORMULA $Ca_2Al_2FeO(SiO_4)(Si_2O_7)(OH)$
- **COLOR** pistachio green to yellowish green to dark gray
- **HARDNESS** 6–7 • **CLEAVAGE** perfect, 1 direction lengthwise
- **FRACTURE** uneven • **STREAK** colorless to gray • **LUSTER** greasy
- **OTHER** transparent to translucent; brittle

10s. spotters

Epidote, commonly found in low-grade metamorphic rocks, is often found with minerals such as hornblende and actinolite. It may also fill the cracks and cavities of basalts. Epidote is usually pistachio green, but can appear as different colors when rotated. The word "epidote" is also used to describe a group of minerals that share the same crystal structure but have different amounts of aluminum and iron. The group includes the mineral epidote.

CRYSTALS CAN BE COLUMNAR, OR SLENDER AND LONG, WITH STRIATIONS.

NAME GAME

In epidote crystals, one side of the prism is usually larger than the other. Its name comes from the Greek word *epidosis*, which means "addition" and refers to that extra size. The only real use of the mineral epidote has been as a gemstone. It is sometimes made into beads and worn as jewelry.

10s. spotters

ZOISITE

CHEMICAL FORMULA $Ca_2Al_3Si_3O_{12}(OH)$
- **COLOR** gray, yellowish brown, greenish, pink, blue • **HARDNESS** 6–6.5
- **CLEAVAGE** good, 1 direction lengthwise • **FRACTURE** uneven to rounded, like a scallop shell • **STREAK** white • **LUSTER** glassy, pearly on cleavage
- **OTHER** transparent to translucent

Zoisite is a member of the epidote group. Although some varieties of this mineral are brightly colored, it most often occurs in muted tones, such as light brown, yellowish green, and gray. Brown zoisite can be turned blue by heating. Zoisite is typically found in metamorphic rocks.

HAS A SINGLE CLEAVAGE PLANE

ITS CRYSTALS HAVE GROOVES CALLED STRIATIONS.

TANZANITE

Tanzanite is a type of zoisite. Its blue or purplish blue color comes from an element called vanadium. It is found only in a small area in Tanzania, East Africa.

EXPERT'S CIRCLE

ZIRCON

CHEMICAL FORMULA $ZrSiO_4$
- COLOR **gray, brown, yellow, green, red, colorless** • HARDNESS **7.5**
- CLEAVAGE **indistinct, 2 directions**
- FRACTURE **uneven** • STREAK **colorless**
- LUSTER **glassy, brilliant**
- OTHER **transparent to translucent; fluorescent; brittle**

Zircon is a mineral that's common in both silica-rich intrusive igneous rocks and metamorphic rocks. It can also be found in the grains of some sedimentary rocks, like sandstone. Its crystals are usually small, often occurring as prisms with a pyramid shape on each end. The mineral is commonly brown to reddish brown, but occurs in a variety of colors caused by different chemical impurities. In some varieties, particularly green zircon, the impurities are caused by radioactive elements. Zircon has been mined as a gemstone for two centuries and is one of the few gems that comes close to the diamond in its brilliance.

VERY HARD, WITH GLASSY OR BRILLIANT LUSTER; VERY DENSE. CRYSTALS CAN BE FOUND CONCENTRATED IN STREAMBEDS.

SMALL, PRISMATIC CRYSTALS

10s spotters

ZIRCON

Since the name "zircon" is similar to that of "cubic zirconia," the two are often confused. Cubic zirconia is a material that's made by humans. It looks like a diamond, but is much less expensive. Cubic zirconia and zircon have nothing in common, except that they both contain the element called zirconium and are sometimes colorless.

EXPERT'S CIRCLE

DIG THiS! Zircon is very refractive, which means that light waves bend when passing through the crystals. To get an idea of how this works, fill a clear glass about halfway with water. Then place a pencil diagonally inside. When you look at the pencil through the side of the glass, it should look broken.

OLIVINE

CHEMICAL FORMULA (Mg,Fe)$_2$SiO$_4$
• COLOR pale olive green to yellow-green, brown • HARDNESS 6.5–7 • CLEAVAGE indistinct, 2 directions at right angles
• FRACTURE uneven; rounded, like a scallop shell • STREAK colorless to white
• LUSTER glassy • OTHER transparent to translucent

Olivine is the name for a series of minerals in which magnesium and iron can take the place of each other without actually changing the mineral's structure. Olivine minerals can be found in igneous rocks that are rich in magnesium and iron. This includes basalt, gabbro, and peridotite. Olivine has also been found in meteorites and is thought to be one of the main components of Earth's upper mantle.

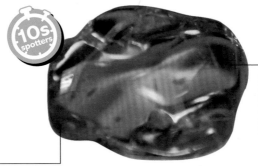

GLASSY LUSTER

YELLOW-GREEN COLOR

be a ROCK HOUND!

The sand of Papakolea Beach in Hawaii contains large quantities of olivine. This gives it a green appearance.

FORSTERITE

Forsterite is the name given to olivine that is rich in magnesium. Its chemical composition is Mg_2SiO_4. Forsterite commonly occurs in igneous rocks. The mineral has also been detected in space. In 2006, traces of forsterite were discovered in comet samples that had been collected by a NASA probe. Some scientists believe that chemical compounds in clouds of gas around a forming star might be tiny grains of forsterite.

APPEARS LIGHT GREEN TO YELLOW-GREEN DUE TO MAGNESIUM CONTENT

FAYALITE

Fayalite is the olivine mineral that is rich in iron. Its chemical composition is Fe_2SiO_4. The group was named after Faial, an island located west of Portugal. Like other olivine minerals, fayalite occurs in igneous rocks. Various quantities of fayalite have also been discovered in meteorites. These quantities have ranged from small traces to half the volume of the meteorite.

YELLOW-GREEN TO BROWN IN COLOR DUE TO IRON CONTENT

PERIDOT

Peridot is the gemstone variety of olivine that has been mined for more than 3,500 years. The gemstone can fall anywhere between the iron-rich end of the olivine spectrum and the magnesium end. Its color is determined by the element that's present. For example, iron-rich peridot will appear brown, while the more popular magnesium-rich varieties will appear yellow-green.

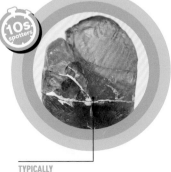

TYPICALLY GREENISH IN COLOR

CHEMICAL FORMULA $Al_2SiO_4(F,OH)_2$
- COLOR colorless, white, yellow, yellow-brown, pink, bluish, greenish • HARDNESS 8 • CLEAVAGE perfect, 1 direction • FRACTURE uneven; somewhat rounded, like a scallop shell
- STREAK colorless • LUSTER glassy
- LUSTER transparent to translucent

Topaz is a silicate mineral that contains aluminum and fluorine. It forms in igneous rocks—particularly in the cavities of granite and rhyolite and in pegmatite. Topaz also occurs in hydrothermal ore deposits. Its crystals can be very large and are usually in the shape of prisms. Topaz is very hard, so when rocks that contain the mineral are weathered in streams, it often remains intact. For this reason, topaz can be found in some streambeds.

COLORS RANGE FROM PALE BLUE TO RED.

10s. spotters

→ LOOK FOR THIS
Don't be fooled by the phrase "smoky topaz." There is no such thing! The phrase is sometimes used to describe smoky quartz. Since quartz is less expensive than topaz, some dishonest dealers may fool people into believing that they are buying more expensive brown-colored topaz.

CRYSTALS OFTEN PRISMATIC, WITH STRIATIONS, OR GROOVES, THAT RUN LENGTHWISE

EXPERT'S CIRCLE

IMPERIAL TOPAZ

While topaz is found in the U.S. states of New Hampshire, Colorado, and Utah, there are also deposits around the world. The state of Minas Gerais, in Brazil, is the most important source of topaz gemstones in the world. A highly prized yellow-orange to orange-brown variety known as imperial topaz is found here.

TITANITE

CHEMICAL FORMULA CaTiSiO$_5$
- COLOR brown to black, yellow, gray, green • HARDNESS
5–5.5 • CLEAVAGE distinct in 2 directions parallel to
prism faces • FRACTURE rounded, like a scallop shell
- STREAK white • LUSTER glassy, resinous, brilliant
- OTHER transparent to translucent

Titanite is a silicate mineral that
contains calcium and titanium. Its
crystals are often wedge-shaped
and sometimes exhibit twinning.
This means that two crystals grow
outward from the same base—like
mirror images of one another, or
twins. In the case of titanite, the
"twin" crystals often are shaped like
deflated footballs. Titanite usually
occurs in silica-rich igneous rocks,
especially granite and pegmatite,
and in some metamorphic rocks,
including gneiss and schist.

GLASSY
LUSTER

WEDGE-SHAPED
CRYSTALS

NAME GAME

If you look up the word "titanite," you'll
likely come across the word "sphene."
"Sphene," which comes from the Greek
word for "wedge-shaped," was an alter-
nate name for this mineral. In 1982, the
name was change to titanite to reflect
the presence of titanium in the mineral.

ANDALUSITE

CHEMICAL FORMULA Al$_2$SiO$_5$
- COLOR white, gray, pink, reddish brown, olive green
- HARDNESS 7.5 • CLEAVAGE good, 2 directions at almost right
angles • FRACTURE rounded like a scallop shell to uneven
- STREAK colorless • LUSTER glassy, dull • OTHER transparent
to translucent

Andalusite is an aluminum silicate that
commonly forms crystals in the shape
of square prisms. One variety, called
chiastolite, forms cross-shaped or
checkerboard patterns within the mineral. Andalusite is most often found
in low-temperature metamorphic rocks, such as gneiss and schist.
Although rare, it can occur in some igneous rocks as well.

OFTEN HAS SQUARE,
PRISMATIC CRYSTALS

GLASSY
LUSTER

SILLIMANITE

CHEMICAL FORMULA Al$_2$SiO$_5$
- COLOR grayish white, brown, greenish brown
- HARDNESS 6–7 • CLEAVAGE perfect, 1 direction lengthwise
- FRACTURE uneven, splintery • STREAK colorless
- LUSTER glassy, silky • OTHER transparent to translucent

Sillimanite is a mineral that has the same chemical composition as andalusite and kyanite, but a different crystal structure. Sillimanite usually occurs as fibrous masses, but can sometimes form long, thin, prismatic crystals. The mineral can appear yellowish green, dark green, or blue when looked at from different angles. Sillimanite is usually found in high-temperature, aluminum-rich metamorphic rocks, such as schist and gneiss.

HARDNESS

USUALLY FIBROUS

GLASSY OR SILKY LUSTER

be a ROCK HOUND!

Sillimanite is the state mineral of Delaware, U.S.A., where it can be found in large masses as boulders.

USUALLY BLUE OR BLUE-GRAY

KYANITE

CHEMICAL FORMULA Al$_2$SiO$_5$
- COLOR blue, white, colorless, gray, green, nearly black
- HARDNESS varies on crystal face: lengthwise, 4–5; crosswise, 6–7 • CLEAVAGE perfect, 1 direction lengthwise; good in a second direction • FRACTURE splintery • STREAK colorless • LUSTER glassy
- OTHER transparent to translucent

GLASSY LUSTER

CAN FORM LONG, BLADED CRYSTALS

Kyanite is unusual because its hardness can vary depending on how it's scratched. With the end of a key, try scratching it lengthwise. It will have a hardness of 4–5. If you scratch it across the width of its crystals, it's harder, with a measure of 6–7.

Kyanite is an aluminum-bearing mineral that has the same chemical composition as andalusite and sillimanite, but a different crystal structure. Kyanite tends to form crystals that are long, bladed, or tabular. It is often found in metamorphic rocks, such as schist and gneiss, that formed as clay-rich sediments changed.

STAUROLITE

CHEMICAL FORMULA $Fe_2Al_9Si_4O_{22}(OH)_2$
- COLOR yellowish brown, reddish to brownish black; gray when weathered ● HARDNESS 7–7.5 ● CLEAVAGE poor, 1 direction lengthwise ● FRACTURE somewhat rounded, like a scallop shell, to uneven ● STREAK white ● LUSTER glassy, dull
- OTHER transparent to opaque

Staurolite is a medium to dark-colored mineral that's found in medium-grade metamorphic rocks, such as gneiss and schist. The mineral tends to grow two crystals at the same time. These crystals, called "twins," are often at 60-degree angles to each other. But sometimes they are perpendicular and form a cross shape. The crystals have well-developed faces and a glassy luster.

CRYSTALS SOMETIMES FORM A CROSS SHAPE.

be a ROCK HOUND!

Some people call staurolite's twin crystals "fairy crosses" and believe that the crystals bring good luck or have healing qualities. But there is no scientific evidence that supports this claim.

WILLEMITE

CHEMICAL FORMULA Zn_2SiO_4
- COLOR yellow, green, red, brown, white ● HARDNESS 5.5
- CLEAVAGE good, 3 directions ● FRACTURE rounded, like a scallop shell, to uneven ● STREAK white ● LUSTER glassy, resinous ● OTHER transparent to translucent

Willemite is a silicate mineral that is used as a zinc ore and often found in hydrothermal deposits with the minerals calcite and franklinite. It can occur as crystals, grains, or fibers. Willemite usually forms small, short crystals. However, its most defining characteristic is its fluorescence. So, when willemite is placed under short-wave ultraviolet light, it glows.

IT GLOWS UNDER ULTRA-VIOLET LIGHT.

GLASSY OR RESINOUS LUSTER

NAME GAME

Willemite is named after Willem I, who was king of the Netherlands in the early 1800s.

GARNET

CHEMICAL FORMULA $X_3Y_2Si_3O_{12}$; depending on the mineral, X=Ca, Fe^{2+}, Mn, or Mg, and Y=Al, Cr, or Fe^{3+} • COLOR orange, yellow, red, green, blue, purple, pink, brown, black • HARDNESS 6.5–7.5 • CLEAVAGE none; parting sometimes distinct in 6 directions • FRACTURE uneven; rounded, like a scallop shell • STREAK white to colorless • LUSTER glassy • OTHER transparent to opaque

Garnets are a group of minerals that are most often found in metamorphic rocks, but they also can occur in intrusive igneous rocks as well as some sedimentary rocks. When most people hear the word "garnet," they think of a

GLASSY LUSTER

CRYSTALS OFTEN TRANSPARENT

HARDNESS

red gemstone, but garnets can come in many different colors, depending on their chemical composition. Different varieties of garnets form under different temperature and pressure conditions. Because of this, geologists use garnets to understand the history of the rocks that they are found in. Garnets have glassy luster and hardness. The crystals often form dodecahedrons—12-sided solids that look like soccer balls.

USUALLY RED

FRACTURE IS ROUNDED, LIKE A SCALLOP SHELL

OFTEN FOUND AS LOOSE GRAINS IN SEDIMENTS

PYROPE

Pyrope is a type of garnet that contains magnesium and aluminum. It is often found in peridotite, the dominant rock of Earth's mantle. Its name comes from the Greek words *pyr* and *ōps*, which mean "fire" and "eye." The words allude to the mineral's often fiery color.

ALMANDINE

Almandine is the most common type of garnet. It contains iron and aluminum and is often found in metamorphic rocks, such as gneiss and mica schist. Almandine is usually red, with a pink, violet, or black tint. It is named after Alabanda, a historic region in Turkey where the mineral was fashioned into gemstones.

RED, SOMETIMES WITH A PINK OR PURPLE TINT

GLASSY LUSTER

CRYSTALS HAVE WELL-FORMED FACES.

be a ROCK HOUND!

Some almandines are called star garnets because they have a crossing pattern inside them—with four or six rays—that looks like a star. Star garnets are very rare; in North America, they're only found in Idaho—in fact, they're the U.S. state's official gemstone!

GROSSULAR

Grossular is a garnet that contains calcium and aluminum. It can often be found in metamorphic rocks that originated as "dirty" lime-stones—containing sand and different minerals. Grossular is most often green. Its color, combined with the fact that it often occurs in masses, causes some people to mistake this mineral for jade.

HAS A GLASSY LUSTER

FORMS SMALL CRYSTALS THAT CREATE A MASS

Grossular's often green color was the inspiration for its name. It comes from *grossularia*, which means "gooseberries" in Latin. Gooseberries are edible green berries native to many parts of Europe and Asia.

CALCITE

CHEMICAL FORMULA $CaCO_3$

- COLOR white, colorless, gray, yellow, blue, brown, black • HARDNESS 3 • CLEAVAGE perfect, 3 directions; calcite breaks into rhombohedrons
- FRACTURE rarely fractures, but when it does, it is somewhat rounded, like a scallop shell; brittle
- STREAK white • LUSTER glassy • OTHER transparent to translucent; fluorescent under ultraviolet light

Calcite is a common mineral that's made of calcium carbonate, which is the same composition of many sea shells. It can be found in sedimentary, metamorphic, and igneous rocks and is the major rock-forming mineral in limestone and marble. As a major component of limestone and marble, calcite is used as building materials in the construction industry. Calcite is usually clear or white, but can occur in other colors, depending on the elements that are present.

ICELAND SPAR

Iceland spar is a clear, transparent form of calcite that has a glassy luster. It can also refract, or bend, light. If you look at a line drawn on a paper through the crystal, you will see two lines. As its name suggests, the mineral was first discovered in Iceland. However, it can be found in other areas, such as the southwestern United States and parts of China.

EXPERT'S CIRCLE

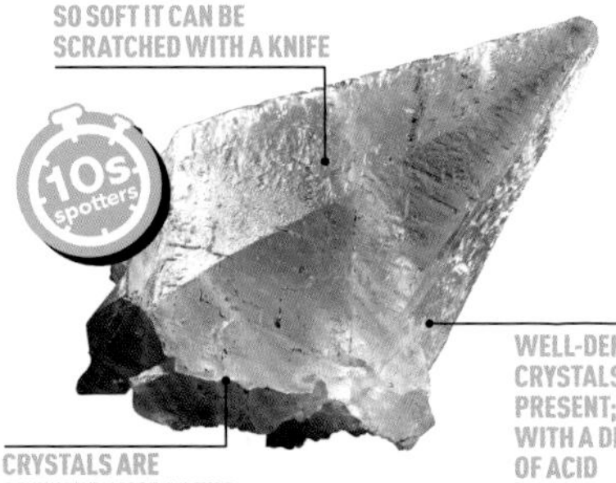

SO SOFT IT CAN BE SCRATCHED WITH A KNIFE

10s spotters

WELL-DEFINED CRYSTALS WHEN PRESENT; FIZZES WITH A DROP OF ACID

CRYSTALS ARE OFTEN TRANSPARENT OR TRANSLUCENT.

The presence of calcite can be detected with an acid test. To see how this works:

DIG THIS!

- Fill a plastic cup halfway with white vinegar. This is your acid.
- Next, drop an eggshell inside. The eggshell contains calcium carbonate. (Make sure you wash your hands after handling the eggshell.)
- Leave the cup alone for about 15 minutes. After the time has passed, look inside the cup. Your eggshell should be fizzy.

DOLOMITE

CHEMICAL FORMULA $CaMg(CO_3)_2$
- COLOR white, colorless, pink, gray, green, brown, black ○ HARDNESS 3.5–4
- CLEAVAGE perfect, 3 directions
- FRACTURE rounded, like a scallop shell; brittle ○ STREAK white ○ LUSTER glassy, pearly ○ OTHER transparent to translucent

Dolomite is a carbonate mineral that is similar to calcite, except that it has magnesium added to its structure. Dolomite crystals are usually long and tabular with curved faces, meaning they are shaped like a tablet or pad. However, some crystals occur in rounded, saddle-shaped clusters. Dolomite can be found in some sedimentary rocks, such as dolostone, and metamorphic rocks, such as marble.

LONG, TABULAR CRYSTALS WITH CURVED FACES

GLASSY OR PEARLY LUSTER

10s. spotters

CRYSTALS OFTEN IN SADDLE-SHAPED CLUSTERS

CALCITE

Sometimes it can be difficult to distinguish dolomite and calcite. An easy way to tell the difference between the two is with an acid test. Calcite will fizz with diluted acid (below); dolomite must be first turned into a powder in order to fizz.

EXPERT'S CIRCLE

be a ROCK HOUND!

Dolomite occurs in some living things. For example, the mineral has been found in the kidney stones of Dalmatians!

ARAGONITE

CHEMICAL FORMULA CaCO$_3$
- COLOR white, gray, colorless, yellow, pale green, violet, brown • HARDNESS 3.5–4 • CLEAVAGE good in 1 direction; poor in 2 others • STREAK white • LUSTER glassy, resinous • OTHER transparent to translucent; fluorescent

Aragonite has the same chemical composition as calcite, but a different crystal structure. Aragonite crystals can be tabular (shaped like a tablet), needlelike, or prismatic, with pyramid-shaped ends. Aragonite precipitates out of, or is left behind by, warm ocean waters. Over time it changes to calcite. Aragonite can also form in metamorphic rocks that experienced high pressure.

FLOS FERRI

Flos ferri is a white, branching type of aragonite that is often formed from minerals precipitating from hot springs. Its crystals may be cylinder-shaped or branched like coral. The mineral's flowery branches and its association with iron are responsible for its name, which means "flower of iron" in Latin.

EXPERT'S CIRCLE

TWINNED CRYSTALS ARE POSSIBLE.

PRISMATIC CRYSTALS

FIZZES UNDER DILUTED ACID

10s spotters

→ LOOK FOR THIS

When you're walking along the beach, look for the shells of mollusks, like oysters and mussels. Inside many mollusk shells you'll find a shiny mother of pearl layer. It's made of aragonite.

CERUSSITE

CHEMICAL FORMULA PbCO$_3$
- COLOR white, gray, colorless, yellow, brown
- HARDNESS 3–3.5 • CLEAVAGE good, 1 direction
- FRACTURE rounded, like a scallop shell; brittle
- STREAK white • LUSTER brilliant, greasy, silky
- OTHER transparent to translucent, fluorescent

Cerussite is a soft mineral that occurs in veins of lead ore. It usually forms when carbonated water reacts with other lead-bearing minerals such as galena. Cerussite crystals occur in a variety of shapes. They can be pyramid-shaped or tabular. Twinned crystals may also occur in shapes such as stars, hearts, or V-shapes.

SOME CRYSTALS FORM IN UNUSUAL SHAPES, SUCH AS STARS

BRILLIANT LUSTER

OFTEN HAS TWINNED CRYSTALS

be a ROCK HOUND!

In spite of its brilliant luster, cerussite is too soft to be used as a gem. Instead, its main use is as a lead ore. This means that lead can be extracted from cerussite and used for various purposes.

MAGNESITE

DULL LUSTER

RARELY FORMS CRYSTALS

be a ROCK HOUND!

Magnesium is mixed with different metals to build a variety of objects, ranging from household appliances to spacecraft.

CHEMICAL FORMULA MgCO3
- COLOR white, yellowish, grayish, brown • HARDNESS 3.5–4.5
- CLEAVAGE perfect in 3 directions, forming rhombohedrons
- FRACTURE somewhat rounded, like a scallop shell; brittle
- STREAK white • LUSTER glassy or dull • OTHER transparent to translucent

Magnesite is a carbonate mineral that contains the element magnesium. It is often found with the mineral brucite in some metamorphic rocks and in mineral deposits left by hot waters circulating under the earth. It can also form in magnesium-rich igneous rocks and may also be found in salt deposits. Magnesite is usually massive, granular, or fibrous and rarely forms crystals.

MALACHITE

CHEMICAL FORMULA $Cu_2CO_3(OH)_2$
- COLOR colorless, emerald green, grass green, dark green
- HARDNESS 3.5–4 • CLEAVAGE perfect, 1 direction
crosswise • FRACTURE rounded, like a scallop shell;
splintery • STREAK light green • LUSTER brilliant,
silky, dull • OTHER translucent

Malachite is a bright-green carbonate mineral that's usually found with other minerals, including azurite and chalcopyrite, in copper ore deposits. It can form thin coatings or icicle-like structures called stalactites. About 4,000 years ago, malachite was a major source of copper. Today, it's only a minor ore of this metallic element.

BRIGHT GREEN; WHEN MASSIVE, IT HAS LIGHT AND DARK GREEN BANDS

RARELY FORMS CRYSTALS AND CAN HAVE A GLOBULAR OR BUBBLY SURFACE

be a ROCK HOUND!

People once believed that malachite had many special powers. This included easing the pain babies experience while teething, curing eye diseases, and protecting someone from getting cursed.

DEEP BLUE COLOR

AZURITE

CHEMICAL FORMULA $Cu_3(CO_3)_2(OH)_2$
- COLOR blue, dark blue • HARDNESS 3.5–4 • CLEAVAGE good,
2 directions • FRACTURE rounded, like a scallop shell
• STREAK blue • LUSTER glassy, dull • OTHER transparent
in thin chips

Azurite is a deep blue carbonate mineral that often occurs near Earth's surface in association with the mineral malachite. Like malachite, it is a copper ore, which means that copper can be extracted from the mineral and used for other purposes. Unlike malachite, azurite commonly forms crystals, which are usually prismatic, wedge-shaped, or tabular.

GLASSY LUSTER

CRYSTALS USUALLY WEDGE-SHAPED, PRISMATIC, OR TABULAR

RHODOCHROSITE

CHEMICAL FORMULA MnCO$_3$
- COLOR pink, rose red, dark red, brown • HARDNESS 3.5–4
- CLEAVAGE perfect in 3 directions, forming a rhombohedron
- FRACTURE uneven • STREAK white • LUSTER glassy or pearly
- OTHER somewhat transparent to translucent

Rhodochrosite is a carbonate mineral that occurs in the fractures and cavities of some metamorphic and sedimentary rocks. Rhodochrosite is known for its striking pink color, which comes from the presence of manganese. But sometimes the manganese is replaced by iron, magnesium, and/or calcium. When this happens, the color of the mineral can become grayish, yellowish, or brown.

DOGTOOTH OR RHOMBOHEDRAL CRYSTALS

OFTEN HOT PINK AND RED

→ **LOOK FOR THIS** Rhodochrosite's color makes it a popular choice for jewelry, but its softness limits the type of jewelry it can be used for. For example, it doesn't work well for rings because they are subject to a lot of wear and tear. Instead, it is a better choice for earrings and necklaces.

SIDERITE

CHEMICAL FORMULA FeCO$_3$
- COLOR light to dark brown, reddish brown, white
- HARDNESS 3.5–4 • CLEAVAGE perfect in 3 directions, forming a rhombohedron • FRACTURE uneven • STREAK white, pale yellow
- LUSTER glassy, pearly, dull • OTHER translucent

Siderite is an ore of iron. It occurs in coal seams and in sedimentary rocks made of clay. It is also present in some igneous and metamorphic rocks. Its crystals can occur in a variety of shapes, but most are curved rhombohedrons—prisms with six faces. Each face is made up of a rhombus, or four-sided shape. Sometimes siderite forms shapes that look like bubbles or grapes.

OFTEN BROWN

CURVED RHOMBOHEDRAL CRYSTALS AND RHOMBOHEDRAL CLEAVAGE

CRYSTALS ARE USUALLY TRANSLUCENT.

→ **LOOK FOR THIS** Some siderite nodules, or masses, in coal fields of Kentucky, U.S.A., have been found with fossils of organisms such as ferns and millipedes.

RUTILE

CHEMICAL FORMULA TiO_2
- COLOR red, reddish brown, black
- HARDNESS 6–6.5 ◦ CLEAVAGE distinct, sometimes good in 2 directions; poor in a third ◦ FRACTURE uneven, brittle
- STREAK white, gray, or pale brown ◦ LUSTER brilliant, somewhat metallic ◦ OTHER translucent to transparent

Rutile is a type of oxide, or a mineral that's formed when oxygen combines with a metal. In the case of rutile, that metal is titanium. Rutile is usually reddish brown. It can be found in small amounts in granite, which is a type of igneous rock, and in gneiss and schist, which are both metamorphic rocks. Rutile also occurs inside some quartz grains as tiny golden, needlelike crystals.

IF INSIDE QUARTZ, CRYSTALS ARE NEEDLELIKE.

CRYSTALS ARE OFTEN TWINNED, WITH GROOVES CALLED STRIATIONS.

NAME GAME

Rutile takes its name from the Latin word *rutilis*, which means "red" or "glowing." It refers to the color of the mineral.

CASSITERITE

CHEMICAL FORMULA SnO_2
- COLOR brown, black; occasionally yellow or gray
- HARDNESS 6–7 ◦ CLEAVAGE distinct ◦ FRACTURE uneven
- STREAK white, light brown ◦ LUSTER greasy or brilliant to dull
- OTHER translucent to transparent

Cassiterite is an oxide that contains tin. In fact, its name comes from the Greek word *kassiteros*, which means "tin." In its pure form, cassiterite is colorless, but when iron is present—as it often is—it appears brown or black. Cassiterite forms in hydrothermal veins deep in Earth's crust. It can be found with minerals such as tourmaline and molybdenite. It also forms in some metamorphic rocks.

REDDISH BROWN OR BLACK DUE TO THE PRESENCE OF IRON

SHORT, PRISMATIC CRYSTALS

PYROLUSITE

UNEVEN FRACTURE; DULL LUSTER

CHEMICAL FORMULA MnO$_2$
- COLOR black to steel gray; sometimes bluish
- HARDNESS 6–6.5 • CLEAVAGE perfect, 1 direction
- FRACTURE splintery, uneven • STREAK black, bluish black • LUSTER metallic to dull

Deep inside Earth, mineral-rich water is heated by magma. Eventually, that hot water dissolves surrounding rock. The dissolved solution then precipitates, or leaves behind, different mineral deposits. Pyrolusite is one—and it's the most important manganese-bearing ore on Earth. Pyrolusite usually occurs in massive clusters and rarely forms crystals.

STREAK IS USUALLY BLACK, RESEMBLING SOOT.

be a ROCK HOUND!

The manganese taken from pyrolusite is used to make a special type of bronze that won't corrode in salt water. It's used to make parts for ships, including propellers.

CHRYSOBERYL

CHEMICAL FORMULA BeAl$_2$O$_4$
- COLOR yellowish green, deep green, greenish white, greenish brown, yellow • HARDNESS 8.5 • CLEAVAGE good in 1 direction; poor in 2 others • FRACTURE rounded, like a scallop shell; uneven • STREAK colorless - white • LUSTER glassy

Chrysoberyl is an extremely hard mineral that contains beryllium and aluminum—only diamond and corundum are harder. Chrysoberyl can be found in igneous rocks, such as granite pegmatite, and several types of metamorphic rocks. It is often found with beryl minerals, which include aquamarine and emerald. However, chrysoberyl's crystal structure is very different from beryl's, so the two are not confused.

TABULAR OR SHORT AND PRISMATIC

CRYSTALS EXHIBIT TWINNING, SOMETIMES IN HEART SHAPES.

→ LOOK FOR THIS

Alexandrite is a rare gemstone variety of chrysoberyl that changes color in different lights. In incandescent light, it appears cherry red!

PYROCHLORE

CHEMICAL FORMULA $(Na,Ca)_2Nb_2O_6(OH,F)$
- COLOR orange, brown, yellowish brown, black
- HARDNESS 5–5.5 · CLEAVAGE distinct · FRACTURE uneven
- STREAK yellowish brown · LUSTER resinous, greasy

Pyrochlore is a major source of niobium, a metal most often used to strengthen materials containing stainless steel and in materials for making jet engines, rockets, oil rigs, and even jewelry. The niobium in pyrochlore is also used in super-conductive magnets for MRI (magnetic resonance imaging) machines, which use magnetic fields to show images inside the human body. Pyrochlore is found in pegmatite and other igneous rocks that are rich in carbonate material and have little silica.

UNEVEN FRACTURE

CRYSTALS ARE USUALLY WELL-FORMED OCTAHE-DRONS, OFTEN TWINNED.

NAME GAME

Some kinds of pyrochlore turn green when heated, giving the mineral its name, which comes from the Greek word *pyr* ("fire") and *chloros* ("green").

METALLIC LUSTER

ILMENITE

CHEMICAL FORMULA $FeTiO_3$
- COLOR black, brownish black · HARDNESS 5–6
- CLEAVAGE none · FRACTURE rounded, like a scallop shell; brittle
- STREAK iron black, brownish black · LUSTER metallic to somewhat metallic · OTHER weakly magnetic

Ilmenite is a type of oxide that contains iron and titanium, for which it is a major source. Ilmenite may also have both magnesium and manganese in it. It is named after the Ilmen Mountains, near Miass, Russia, where it was discovered. Ilmenite usually forms thick, tabular crystals. However, it can also occur in massive clusters or as scattered grains in streambeds. Ilmenite is common in igneous rocks, such as diorite and gabbro.

BROWN OR BLACK, WITH BLACK STREAK

USUALLY TABULAR CRYSTALS

CUPRITE

CHEMICAL FORMULA Cu_2O
- COLOR **ruby red, reddish black, green** · HARDNESS **3.5–4** · CLEAVAGE **poor** · FRACTURE **uneven** · STREAK **brownish red** · LUSTER **somewhat metallic, either brilliant or dull** · OTHER **translucent**

Cuprite is a red copper oxide that's formed by the weathering of copper sulfide minerals. It is often found with native copper, malachite, and calcite. Cuprite is an important ore of copper. It usually occurs as eight-sided crystals, but it can also form cubes, ten-sided crystals, single grains, or earthy masses. One kind of cuprite, nicknamed "plush copper," has fibers so densely packed that the mineral looks velvety.

RELATIVELY SOFT

STREAK IS BROWNISH RED.

CAN FORM EIGHT-SIDED AND CUBIC CRYSTALS

→ **LOOK FOR THIS**
When cuprite is freshly broken, it is usually a bright red color. However, after it has been exposed to the air, it begins to turn a dull, metallic gray color.

DEEP RED COLOR

OFTEN ACCOMPANIED BY DARK FRANKLINITE

Zincite is an ore of the metal zinc, which is used in many industries. Since zinc oxide is white, zincite most likely gets its red color from the presence of manganese.

ZINCITE

CHEMICAL FORMULA $(Zn,Mn)O$
- COLOR **deep red to orange, yellow, or brown** · HARDNESS **4** · CLEAVAGE **perfect, 1 direction** · FRACTURE **rounded, like a scallop shell** · STREAK **orange-yellow** · LUSTER **brilliant, resinous, dull metallic** · OTHER **transparent to translucent**

Zincite is a rare, red mineral. It forms in deposits left by hot, mineral-rich fluids in Earth's crust. It often occurs as masses with other minerals, particularly franklinite and calcite. Zincite rarely forms crystals, but when they do occur, they are often pyramid-shaped. One of the few places to find zincite in North America is in the zinc mines of Franklin, New Jersey, U.S.A.

HEMATITE

CHEMICAL FORMULA Fe_2O_3

- COLOR steel gray, reddish gray, red, brown black
- HARDNESS 5–6 • CLEAVAGE none • FRACTURE uneven, splintery, brittle • STREAK red to brownish red
- LUSTER metallic

Hematite is a common iron oxide that can be found primarily in sedimentary deposits, but may also be found in both metamorphic and igneous rocks. The mineral varies greatly from one specimen to the next. Its color can range from steel gray to bright red, but it always produces a red or reddish-brown streak. Its crystals can resemble thick or thin columns or be shaped like tiny rosettes. Sometimes it occurs as fine-grained masses. Hematite has several uses, but since 70 percent of it is made of iron, its primary use is as an ore of iron.

KIDNEY ORE

Kidney ore is a type of hematite with a bubbly surface. It's a great example of how much hematite can vary in shape from one specimen to the next, based on where it forms.

EXPERT'S CIRCLE

DIFFERENT CRYSTAL SHAPES

VARIETY OF COLORS

10s. spotters

EIGHT-SIDED CRYSTALS

be a ROCK HOUND!

Hematite has been found on the surface of Mars and is gray in color. Experts believe that it may have formed there from hot springs that were active in the planet's distant past.

MAGNETITE

CHEMICAL FORMULA Fe$_2$O$_4$
- COLOR iron black, dark gray
- HARDNESS 5.5–6.5 • CLEAVAGE none
- FRACTURE uneven; somewhat rounded, like a scallop shell • STREAK black
- LUSTER metallic • OTHER magnetic

Magnetite is an iron oxide found in sedimentary, metamorphic, and igneous rocks. It is particularly abundant in igneous rocks, including diorite and gabbro. Magnetite's dark-gray-to-black color and metallic luster causes some people to mistake it for gray hematite. But magnetite is magnetic and has a black streak. Magnetite often forms octahedral crystals. These have eight triangular sides.

10s. spotters

DARK GRAY

BEST IDENTIFIED BY ITS BLACK STREAK AND MAGNETISM

LODESTONE
Regular magnetite is attracted to a magnet. Lodestone, however, is a type of magnetite that acts as an actual magnet. In the photo shown here, iron filings are attracted to lodestone.

EXPERT'S CIRCLE

NAME GAME

Legend has it that magnetite is named after Magnes, an ancient Greek boy whose shoe nails became stuck on a rock containing magnetite. Another theory says that the name comes from the area known as Magnesia, which has large deposits of the stone.

CORUNDUM

CHEMICAL FORMULA Al_2O_3

- COLOR white, gray, brown, deep red, blue, pink, yellow, green • HARDNESS 9 • CLEAVAGE none; often parting in 3 directions • FRACTURE uneven; rounded, like a scallop shell; brittle • STREAK none • LUSTER glassy, brilliant • OTHER transparent to translucent; fluorescent

Corundum is one of the hardest minerals on Earth. Only diamonds are harder. Its hardness is the result of the strong chemical bonds that unite its atoms. Corundum is often white, gray, or brown, but gemstone varieties, which include rubies and sapphires, are more brightly colored. Corundum occurs in high-grade metamorphic rocks, such as gneiss, and in igneous rocks called nepheline syenite pegmatites.

→ LOOK FOR THIS

Some people confuse corundum with plagioclase feldspars (below) because both have striations on some of their crystal faces. Corundum, however, is a much harder mineral.

CRYSTALS OCCUR AS PRISMS WITH HEXAGON-SHAPED FACES OR AS DOUBLE PYRAMIDS.

GROOVES, OR STRIATIONS, ON SOME FACES

10S. spotters

be a ROCK HOUND!

Because of its hardness, corundum is often used as an abrasive.

Laugh Out Loud!

Joke: Why can you never trust atoms?

Answer: They make up everything!

SAPPHIRE

Sapphire is a gemstone variety of corundum. It contains trace amounts of iron and titanium, which give the gemstone its blue color. Other impurities may cause corundum to turn pink, yellow, or green. These gemstones are called "fancy sapphires," though in spite of their name, they are much less valued than the blue variety. Sapphires are often used in jewelry and are the birthstone for the month of September.

USUALLY PRISMS HAVE HEXAGON-SHAPED FACES.

BLUE IS BEST KNOWN COLOR.

be a ROCK HOUND!

The ancient Persians believed that the sky got its color from a sapphire.

DEEP RED COLOR; HEXAGON-SHAPED CRYSTALS

→ LOOK FOR THIS

In the book *The Wonderful Wizard of Oz*, by Frank Baum, Dorothy's slippers are silver. They are ruby red in the film because executives thought they'd look better on screen. See them in the Smithsonian National Museum of American History in Washington, D.C., U.S.A.

RUBY

Like sapphires, rubies are a gemstone form of corundum. They have a deep red color that comes from the presence of chromium. Rubies and other gem-quality corundum usually form in metamorphic rocks, such as schist and gneiss, and in igneous rocks such as syenite. However, these gems are rarely mined from the rocks in which they form because they often break during the process. Instead, natural weathering processes free the rubies from their rocks and carry them into streams, where they are collected.

ROCK STARS:
Gemstones

Many Native Americans value turquoise and use it as a gemstone in decorative arts. This Navajo bracelet is made of turquoise.

WEAPONS WITH STYLE

In some cultures, weapons were decorated with gemstones. This dagger was created in India in the early 1600s. It is made of gold and decorated with rubies and colored glass.

Gemstones

Gemstones are special stones that are prized for their beauty and rarity. They are cut and polished and then used as jewelry or other decorative items. Gemstones include some minerals and rocks as well as petrified materials—matter that came from a living thing, and then over time, hardened into stone. To transform a rough stone into a magnificent gem, an expert called a lapidary first cuts the stone with a special saw. Then the stone is ground against a coarse spinning wheel into one of several shapes, including a heart, oval, or pear. The final step is to buff the gemstone against a less coarse spinning wheel until it shines.

CROWN JEWELS

Crowns with royal jewels are on display at ancient Hradcany Castle in Prague, in the Czech Republic. The crown in the background rests on the thousand-year-old skull of St. Wenceslas.

DOG TIARA

In 2009, a jewelry designer in Thailand crafted an emerald-and-diamond tiara for his pet dog. It was worth $4.2 million!

SPINEL

CHEMICAL FORMULA $MgAl_2O_4$
- **COLOR** red, green, blue, brown, black • **HARDNESS** 7.5–8
- **CLEAVAGE** none • **FRACTURE** uneven; rounded, like a scallop shell; brittle • **STREAK** white • **LUSTER** glassy, dull • **OTHER** transparent to translucent; sometimes fluorescent

"Spinel" is the name of a gemstone-quality, magnesium-rich aluminum oxide that forms in some igneous rocks, such as gabbro, and in certain metamorphic rocks. Spinel can occur as grains or masses, but it most often occurs with octahedral (eight-sided) crystals. Sometimes the mineral is confused with sapphire or ruby because of its hardness and bright-red or blue color.

GAHNITE

Gahnite is a mineral that is related to spinel, except it has zinc instead of magnesium in its chemical composition. Although the mineral is usually dark green or black or even blue, it has a gray streak. Gahnite was named after John Gottlieb Gahn, a Swedish chemist and mineralogist.

EXPERT'S CIRCLE

OCTAHEDRAL CRYSTALS

HARDNESS

RED OR BLUE COLOR

10s spotters

CHROMITE

CHEMICAL FORMULA $FeCr_2O_4$
- COLOR brown, black • HARDNESS 5.5 • CLEAVAGE none; indistinct, parting in 4 directions • FRACTURE uneven; rounded, like a scallop shell; brittle • STREAK dark brown • LUSTER metallic, dull
- OTHER may be slightly magnetic

Chromite is an oxide mineral similar to spinel and is composed of iron, chromium, and oxygen. It rarely forms crystals. It's often found in intrusive igneous rocks rich in magnesium and iron and in sediments from those rocks.

BROWN OR BLACK; RARELY HAS CRYSTALS

GOETHITE

CHEMICAL FORMULA $FeO(OH)$
- COLOR yellowish brown, dark brown, black • HARDNESS 5–5.5
- CLEAVAGE perfect, 1 direction lengthwise • FRACTURE uneven, splintery
- STREAK yellow, yellowish brown • LUSTER somewhat metallic, brilliant to dull

THREADLIKE CRYSTALS; SMALL CRYSTALS APPEAR YELLOWISH BROWN; LARGE CRYSTALS APPEAR DARK.

Goethite is an iron-rich mineral that often forms when other iron-rich minerals, such as pyrite, combine with oxygen and break down through a chemical weathering process. Goethite is usually found with minerals like calcite and quartz. Together they form crusts on the weathered minerals.

LIMONITE

CHEMICAL FORMULA $FeO(OH) \cdot nH_2O_4$
- COLOR yellow, brown • HARDNESS 4–5.5 • CLEAVAGE none
- FRACTURE rounded, like a scallop shell; uneven; splintery
- STREAK yellowish brown • LUSTER glassy, silky, dull

Limonite is a form of goethite and an ore of iron that creates a crust on iron-bearing minerals, such as hematite and pyrite, when they are weathered. It also can be found in soils. Limonite rarely forms crystals. It is used to make paints.

YELLOW OR BROWN; FORMS COMPACT MASSES

BAUXITE

CHEMICAL FORMULA gibbsite: $AlOH_3$; boehmite: $AlO(OH)$; diaspore: $HAlO_2$ • COLOR white, gray, yellow, red, brown • HARDNESS 1–3 • CLEAVAGE none • FRACTURE uneven • STREAK white • LUSTER dull, earthy

Bauxite forms from the chemical weathering of other aluminum-rich minerals and often contains the minerals gibbsite, boehmite, and diaspore. It is the principal ore of aluminum in the world today, which makes it a valuable resource for use in manufacturing. Bauxite often forms nodules—small, round masses—in the soil and frequently has a pisolitic structure. This means that it is made up of many grains no larger than the size of a pea.

DIASPORE

Diaspore is one of the three minerals that usually form bauxite. Diaspore can be colorless, white, grayish, light brown, yellowish, lilac, or pink, and it usually has small, tabular crystals. In some locations, well-developed diaspore crystals are cut and used as gemstones. The mineral's name comes from the Greek word *diaspora*, which means "scattering." This is because of the way diaspore crackles when under intense heat.

EXPERT'S CIRCLE

PISOLITIC STRUCTURE OF MANY GRAINS

SOFT MATERIAL

10s spotters

DIG THiS! Because it's lightweight, it doesn't rust, and it's a good conductor of heat, aluminum is used in everything from foil and beverage containers to pots and utensils. Check out its many uses for yourself: Grab a pad and pencil and head for the kitchen. Make a list of all the pots, pans, and bowls in your cabinets and on the stove that look like they contain aluminum. (Don't forget the aluminum foil!) You'll see just how much aluminum you use on a day-to-day basis!

BRUCITE

CHEMICAL FORMULA $Mg(OH)_2$
- COLOR white, colorless, grayish, bluish, greenish
- HARDNESS 2–2.5   • CLEAVAGE perfect, 1 direction
- FRACTURE uneven   • STREAK white
- LUSTER waxy to glassy; pearly

Brucite is a magnesium hydroxide. It occurs with the minerals calcite and wollastonite in some igneous rocks. It may also occur with magnesite, talc, and aragonite in some metamorphic rocks. It is usually white, but can also be pale green, gray, or blue. It was named for Archibald Bruce, the American mineralogist who first described it.

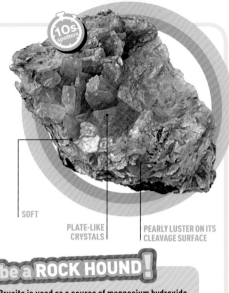

SOFT

PLATE-LIKE CRYSTALS

PEARLY LUSTER ON ITS CLEAVAGE SURFACE

be a ROCK HOUND!

Brucite is used as a source of magnesium hydroxide, which is used in medical products such as laxatives like milk of magnesia. Because of its high melting point, it is also used as insulation in devices such as kilns used for making pottery.

FRANKLINITE

CHEMICAL FORMULA $(Zn,Mn,Fe^{2+})(Fe^{3+},Mn^{3+})2O^4$
- COLOR black   • HARDNESS 5.5–6.5
- CLEAVAGE none; indistinct, parting in 4 directions
- FRACTURE rounded, like a scallop shell   • STREAK black, brownish black, reddish brown   • LUSTER metallic dull

Franklinite is an iron oxide that usually has some amounts of manganese. On a worldwide scale, franklinite is a rare mineral. However, large amounts can be found in the zinc deposits of two U.S. towns in New Jersey— Sterling Hill and Franklin (where it was discovered). There, it typically occurs with calcite, willemite, and zincite. It's brown to black, usually with octahedral (eight-sided) crystals.

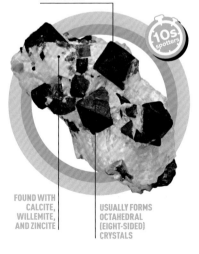

BROWN-TO-BLACK COLOR

FOUND WITH CALCITE, WILLEMITE, AND ZINCITE

USUALLY FORMS OCTAHEDRAL (EIGHT-SIDED) CRYSTALS

BORNITE

CHEMICAL FORMULA Cu_5FeS_4
- COLOR **copper red to brown with deep blue, purple**
- HARDNESS **3** • CLEAVAGE **none** • FRACTURE **uneven; rounded, like a scallop shell** • STREAK **grayish black** • LUSTER **metallic**

Bornite is a common copper-iron mineral that has splashes of iridescent purple, blue, and red mixed with its natural coppery color. Bornite occurs mainly in metamorphic and igneous rocks with other copper ore deposits that have minerals such as chalcopyrite, pyrite, marcosite, and quartz. It is classified as a sulfide, which is a mineral that forms when sulfur combines with a metal or semimetal—in this case, copper.

COLORFUL TARNISH WHEN IT COMBINES WITH OXYGEN

OCCURS WITH OTHER COPPER MINERALS; RARELY FORMS CRYSTALS

NAME GAME

Bornite's colorful tarnish has earned this mineral the nickname "peacock ore."

DARK GRAY LEAD COLOR WITH A METALLIC LUSTER; RELATIVELY SOFT YET BRITTLE

→ LOOK FOR THIS
Chalcocite has a metallic luster, but when exposed to light, it will become dull over time.

CHALCOCITE

CHEMICAL FORMULA Cu_2S
- COLOR **dark lead-gray** • HARDNESS **2.5–3**
- CLEAVAGE **poor, 1 direction** • FRACTURE **rounded, like a scallop shell; brittle** • STREAK **dark gray to black**
- LUSTER **metallic**

Chalcocite is considered an important ore of copper. In fact, the mineral gets its name from the Greek word *chalkos*, which means "copper." Chalcocite usually forms in low-temperature hydrothermal veins or fractures in Earth's crust, and in basalt, a type of igneous rock. It also is produced when the mineral bornite goes through physical changes, or alterations.

COVELLITE

CHEMICAL FORMULA **CuS**
- **COLOR** dark blue or indigo; often iridescent in yellow, red, or purple • **HARDNESS** 1.5–2 • **CLEAVAGE** perfect, 1 direction
- **FRACTURE** uneven, brittle • **STREAK** lead gray to black
- **LUSTER** somewhat metallic

Covellite is a copper-sulfide mineral with a distinctive dark blue or indigo color and a yellow, red, or purple shimmer. Covellite usually occurs in massive clusters. Well-formed crystals are rare, but when crystals are present, they appear as thin, tabular, and hexagon-shaped plates. Covellite typically forms with other copper-mineral deposits in hydrothermal deposits and in some metamorphic rocks.

TYPICALLY DARK BLUE; PLATE-LIKE; QUITE SOFT

FOUND WITH OTHER COPPER MINERALS SUCH AS BORNITE

NAME GAME

Covellite is named after Niccolo Covelli, the mineralogist who discovered it in 1832 on Mount Vesuvius, the famous volcano that destroyed Pompeii in 79 c.e.

SPHALERITE

CHEMICAL FORMULA **ZnS**
- **COLOR** colorless, yellow, brown, red, green, black
- **HARDNESS** 3.5–4 • **CLEAVAGE** perfect, 6 directions
- **FRACTURE** rounded, like a scallop shell; brittle
- **STREAK** light brown • **LUSTER** brilliant, somewhat metallic

Sphalerite is a common zinc sulfide found in sedimentary, metamorphic, and igneous rocks. In the United States, it is found in New Jersey and Missouri, where it often occurs with galena. It's mined primarily as an ore of zinc and is sometimes used as a gemstone. Pure sphalerite is white and rare. Instead, it usually contains some iron, which gives it color, such as brown, green, or red. When crystals form, they are pyramids or dodecahedrons (12-sided structures).

REDDISH BROWN OR GREEN COLOR; METALLIC LUSTER

be a ROCK HOUND!

Sphalerite has been found in meteorites and in moon rocks.

GALENA

CHEMICAL FORMULA PbS • COLOR dark lead-gray • HARDNESS 2.5 • CLEAVAGE perfect, 3 directions at right angles • FRACTURE somewhat rounded, like a scallop shell • STREAK dark lead-gray • LUSTER metallic; dull when exposed to the atmosphere

Galena is the most common lead mineral, and it is most often found in hydrothermal replacement deposits that also contain copper and zinc ores. It can also be found in some metamorphic rocks, such as skarn. Galena has been a popular ore of lead for thousands of years. To extract the lead, many people simply place the mineral in a fire. The fire decomposes the galena, leaving the leftover lead in the ashes. This process is called smelting.

→ LOOK FOR THIS

Because of its lead-gray color and metallic luster, galena is sometimes confused with another sulfide mineral called stibnite. Stibnite, however, doesn't contain lead. Instead, it has an element called antimony. Galena and stibnite may look alike on the surface, but stibnite has long, bladed crystals, while galena's are short and many-sided. Also, stibnite is softer than galena, and its crystals will bend! Here's the clincher: Galena is so dense that a piece of it weighs twice the weight of an equal-size piece of stibnite.

CRYSTALS USUALLY SHAPED LIKE CUBES OR OCTAHEDRONS

10s spotters

LEAD-GRAY COLOR

VERY DENSE

be a ROCK HOUND!

In 2004, researchers studied snow on Venus and developed a theory that it could be made partly of galena.

CINNABAR

CHEMICAL FORMULA HgS
- **COLOR** bright red, purplish red, brownish red
- **HARDNESS** 2–2.5 • **CLEAVAGE** perfect, 3 directions
- **FRACTURE** somewhat rounded, like a scallop shell, to uneven • **STREAK** scarlet to brownish red • **LUSTER** brilliant to dull

Cinnabar, a mercury-sulfide mineral, is instantly recognizable by its bright red color. It can be found around hot springs or near areas where there has been recent volcanic activity. Cinnabar usually occurs as massive or granular clusters. Crystals are uncommon. When they do form, they can be tabular, prismatic, or shaped like a rhombohedron (a solid figure whose faces are six equal rhombuses).

ROUNDED FRACTURE

10s spotters

SCARLET TO BROWNISH RED COLOR

→ **LOOK FOR THIS**
Cinnabar's bright red color is similar to that of cuprite (below). However, cuprite is a much harder mineral.

NAME GAME

The name "cinnabar" comes from the Persian word *zinjirfrah* and the Arabic word *zibjafr,* which mean "dragon's blood." The name refers to the mineral's color.

CHALCOPYRITE

CHEMICAL FORMULA $CuFeS_2$ • COLOR brass yellow, golden yellow, deep blue, purple, black when tarnished • HARDNESS 3.5–4 • CLEAVAGE poor, 1 direction • FRACTURE uneven, brittle • STREAK greenish black • LUSTER metallic

Chalcopyrite is a very common copper and iron sulfide mineral that's usually deposited by hot liquids into hydrothermal veins in igneous rock. There, it can be found with other minerals, including pyrite, chalcocite, and gold. It can also be found in certain metamorphic rocks, such as skarn and schist. Chalcopyrite often forms pyramid-like crystals that can measure up to four inches (10 cm) long on one side.

→ LOOK FOR THIS

Pyrite (below) is an iron sulfide that looks similar to and is sometimes found with chalcopyrite. This may cause some people to confuse the two. However, pyrite is a harder mineral and less yellow in color. In addition, grooves called striations appear in different directions on chalcopyrite's crystal faces, while on pyrite they are parallel.

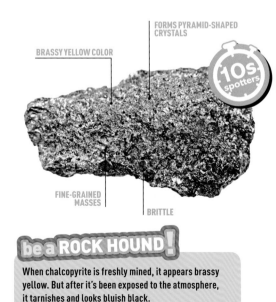

FORMS PYRAMID-SHAPED CRYSTALS

BRASSY YELLOW COLOR

10S spotters

FINE-GRAINED MASSES

BRITTLE

be a ROCK HOUND!

When chalcopyrite is freshly mined, it appears brassy yellow. But after it's been exposed to the atmosphere, it tarnishes and looks bluish black.

REALGAR

CHEMICAL FORMULA **AsS**
- COLOR **deep red to orange; becomes yellow when exposed to light** • HARDNESS **1.5–2**
- CLEAVAGE **good, 1 direction lengthwise**
- FRACTURE **rounded, like a scallop shell**
- STREAK **orange-yellow**
- LUSTER **brilliant to dull**

Realgar is a bright-red or orange mineral that forms in hydrothermal veins deep inside Earth. It often occurs with other minerals, such as cinnabar, stibnite, and orpiment. It can also be found on the surface near active volcanic vents, hot springs, and geysers. Realgar usually forms as coarse or fine granular masses. Crystals are rarely present. When they do occur, they are short and prismatic and have grooves called striations. Realgar is used as an ore for the element arsenic.

BRIGHT-RED OR ORANGE COLOR

10s spotters

WHEN CRYSTALS FORM, THEY ARE PRISMATIC.

⚠ DANGER!

Realgar is an ore of arsenic, which is poisonous. If you break realgar, never inhale the dust. Never hold the mineral anywhere near your mouth or nose, and always wash your hands after handling it.

→ **LOOK FOR THIS**
Realgar can easily be confused with cinnabar. Both minerals are a similar color and are often found together. However, cinnabar is slightly harder and feels heavier when held.

ORPIMENT

CHEMICAL FORMULA As_2S_3
- COLOR lemon yellow, orange
- HARDNESS 1.5–2 ○ CLEAVAGE good, 1 direction
- FRACTURE uneven; can be cut into pieces ○ STREAK lemon yellow, orange ○ LUSTER resinous (smooth); pearly on the cleavage ○ OTHER translucent to transparent

Orpiment is an arsenic-sulfide mineral that often occurs in hot-spring deposits, veins in Earth's crust, and in openings near volcanoes. It is sometimes found with stibnite and realgar. Orpiment is soft and yellow and often forms layers or sheets similar to mica. It was once used as a pigment to make gold-colored paint. However, when poisonous arsenic was discovered in it, the practice was abandoned.

CLEAVAGE HAS A PEARLY LUSTER.

BRIGHT YELLOW COLOR

be a ROCK HOUND!

Orpiment, like other arsenic minerals, gives off a garlic odor when heated.

STIBNITE

CHEMICAL FORMULA Sb_2S_3
- COLOR lead gray to silver gray; sometimes has a black tarnish ○ HARDNESS 2 ○ CLEAVAGE perfect, 1 direction lengthwise ○ FRACTURE uneven; crystals range from slightly flexible to brittle ○ STREAK dark gray to black ○ LUSTER metallic

Stibnite is a sulfide mineral that's lead gray to silver gray in color. When exposed to light, stibnite develops a black tarnish over time. It often occurs with minerals such as galena, cinnabar, realgar, orpiment, pyrite, and quartz. It can be found in hot-spring deposits and in some veins in Earth's crust.

LEAD GRAY

LONG, NEEDLELIKE CRYSTALS APPEAR BENT OR TWISTED

be a ROCK HOUND!

Stibnite is the most important ore of the element antimony and was used along with galena to make a powder called kohl in the ancient Middle East. This powder was used primarily as eyeliner.

PYRITE

CHEMICAL FORMULA FeS_2
- COLOR pale yellow to brass yellow; sometimes has a brown tarnish when exposed to light
- HARDNESS 6–6.5 • CLEAVAGE none
- FRACTURE uneven, brittle • STREAK greenish black
- LUSTER metallic

Pyrite is the most common sulfide mineral. It contains iron and has a brassy yellow color when mined, but turns darker when exposed to oxygen. It can be found in many different rock types, including veins in both igneous and metamorphic rocks, and in sedimentary rocks, such as shale and coal. Pyrite crystals can be cubic, eight-sided, twelve-sided, massive or granular, or disk-shaped. It is often used as a source of both sulfur and iron. Pyrite is often called "fool's gold" because its brassy color and metallic luster cause people to mistake it for gold. But it's not as soft or as dense as gold. Pyrite will crack or shatter if struck, but gold will bend.

NAME GAME

The name "pyrite" comes from the Greek word *pyr*, which means "fire." The name was given to the mineral because it gives off a spark when struck against certain metals. This was sometimes used to start a fire. If you strike pyrite with a steel knife blade, it will often make a spark.

10s spotters

CUBIC CRYSTALS

BRASSY YELLOW COLOR

PARALLEL STRIATIONS ON ITS CRYSTAL FACES

Laugh Out Loud!

Joke: Why was gold afraid of pyrite?

Answer: Because pyrite had a mean streak.

MARCASITE

CHEMICAL FORMULA FeS_2
- **COLOR** pale, brass yellow to white
- **HARDNESS** 6–6.5 • **CLEAVAGE** distinct, 2 directions
- **FRACTURE** uneven, brittle • **STREAK** gray-green to brownish black • **LUSTER** metallic

Marcasite is an iron-sulfide mineral similar to pyrite. Both have the same chemical composition and tarnish when exposed to oxygen. But marcasite is different in its crystal habit, or shape. Its crystals are often pyramid-shaped or tabular (shaped like a tablet). They can also be twinned and curved. Marcasite is found near Earth's surface and often precipitates from solutions that have flowed through beds of shale, clay, limestone, or chalk. It's also in hydrothermal veins and some metamorphic rocks, such as skarn.

BRASSY YELLOW COLOR

CRYSTALS OFTEN TABULAR OR PYRAMID-SHAPED

be a ROCK HOUND!

Marcasite can be found in the shape of fossils from ancient sea creatures called ammonites. The mineral gradually replaces the fossil shell as it weathers away and takes on the shell's spiral shape.

BLUISH GRAY COLOR

CRYSTALS ARE OFTEN TABULAR AND HEXAGON-SHAPED OR IN LAYERED MASSES.

MOLYBDENITE

CHEMICAL FORMULA MoS_2
- **COLOR** bluish lead-gray • **HARDNESS** 1–1.5
- **CLEAVAGE** perfect, 1 direction • **FRACTURE** uneven
- **STREAK** grayish black; greenish • **LUSTER** metallic

Molybdenite is a sulfide mineral that contains molybdenum, an element that's used in super-strong steels. Molybdenite itself is usually blue-gray and occurs in igneous rocks, such as granite and pegmatite, and in veins in Earth's crust. It is also found in some metamorphic rocks. Molybdenite often forms tabular, hexagon-shaped crystals that bend easily and may feel greasy.

BARITE

CHEMICAL FORMULA $BaSO_4$
- COLOR white, gray, colorless, shades of yellow, brown, red, blue • HARDNESS 3–3.5
- CLEAVAGE perfect in 1 direction; good in a second; distinct in a third • FRACTURE uneven
- STREAK white • LUSTER glassy, pearly

Barite is a dense, heavy mineral that's a member of the sulfate group. Sulfate minerals are classified as having sulfur and oxygen combined with a variety of other elements. In barite, that other element is barium. Barite is the most common barium-bearing mineral and occurs in veins of lead and zinc ore, as well as in sedimentary rocks, clay deposits, marine deposits, and some igneous rocks, especially hydrothermal replacement veins.

10s spotters

FORMS THIN -TO-THICK TABULAR CRYSTALS OR PRISMS

DENSE, LIGHT-COLORED MINERAL

COCKSCOMB BARITE

Although barite crystals are usually tabular, they may also appear in a cockscomb form. "Cockscomb" is a term that's used to describe clusters of plate-like crystals. The term suggests that they form a shape that resembles the comb, or crest, on top of a rooster's head.

EXPERT'S CIRCLE

NAME GAME

A measurement called specific gravity (SG) is given to all minerals. The SG of a mineral notes how heavy a mineral is by its relative weight to water. Barite has an SG of 4.5, meaning it's 4.5 times heavier than water. This is considered heavy, especially for a nonmetallic mineral. SG is what gives barite its name, which comes from the Greek word *barys*, meaning "heavy."

CELESTINE

CHEMICAL FORMULA $SrSO_4$
- COLOR white, colorless, blue, reddish
- HARDNESS 3–3.5 ○ CLEAVAGE perfect in 1 direction; good in a second; distinct in a third ○ FRACTURE uneven, brittle
- STREAK white ○ LUSTER glassy, pearly
- OTHER transparent to translucent

Celestine, also called celestite, is a sulfate mineral that gets its name from the Latin word *coelestis*, which means "heavenly" and refers to its often light blue color. Celestine typically forms long, tabular crystals that can grow up to 30 inches (75 cm). The crystals can also be bladed or form long, stretched-out pyramids. Celestine forms in the cavities of sedimentary rocks in salt deposits that were left by mineral-rich water.

TABULAR, TRANSPARENT CRYSTALS

USUALLY BLUE IN COLOR

be a ROCK HOUND!

Celestine contains strontium, a silvery white or yellow element that turns red when burned. Strontium gives fireworks a bright red color.

COLORLESS, WHITE, OR GRAY

CRYSTALS OFTEN FIBROUS AND HAVE WOOLLY APPEARANCE

EPSOMITE

CHEMICAL FORMULA $MgSO_4 \bullet 7H_2O$
- COLOR white, colorless, gray ○ HARDNESS 2–2.5
- CLEAVAGE good in 1 direction; poor in another
- FRACTURE rounded, like a scallop shell ○ STREAK white
- LUSTER glassy, dull ○ OTHER tastes salty or bitter

Epsomite is a magnesium-sulfate mineral that contains water molecules and is found on every continent. It was first discovered around hot springs in the English town of Epsom. Often it is a chemical precipitate, meaning that it is left behind, or precipitated from, a liquid solution. It usually forms as a woolly or powdery coating on the walls of some mines. It can also be found with coal in weathered, magnesium-rich rocks.

GYPSUM

CHEMICAL FORMULA $CaSO_4 \cdot 2H_2O$
- COLOR white, colorless, gray, yellow, red, brown
- HARDNESS 1.5–2 • CLEAVAGE perfect in 1 direction; distinct in 2 others • FRACTURE rounded, like a scallop shell; splintery • STREAK white • LUSTER glassy; pearly on cleavage surfaces • OTHER transparent to translucent

Gypsum is a calcium sulfate, and like epsomite, it contains water molecules. It occurs in deposits left by lakes and seas that have evaporated and can be found in some sedimentary rocks. Gypsum is often white or colorless, but can occur in other colors if impurities are present. Crystal shapes vary from one variety of the mineral to the next. They may be fine-grained or shaped like rosettes, horns, or swords. Gypsum is used to make plaster and cement products for buildings.

SELENITE GYPSUM

Selenite gypsum is a transparent and colorless form of gypsum that can form swordlike crystals. Many fine examples of this specimen can be found in the Cueva de los Cavos, or Cave of Swords, in the Naica Mine of Chihuahua, Mexico.

ALABASTER GYPSUM OCCURS IN FINE-GRAINED MASSES.

MANY FORMS OF GYPSUM, INCLUDING THIS ALABASTER VARIETY, ARE WHITE AND TRANSLUCENT.

EXPERT'S CIRCLE

DIG THiS!

When salt water evaporates, it can leave behind mineral deposits. To see how this is done, make your own saltwater crystals using Epsom salts!

- Grab an aluminum pie pan. Cut a piece of black construction paper into a circle that's the size of the pan bottom. Place the circle into the pan.
- Stir two tablespoons (30 mL) of Epsom salts into one cup (250 mL) of warm water until dissolved.
- Pour the saltwater mixture into the pie pan. Place the pan by a window for three days. Then check out the crystals that have formed!

ANHYDRITE

CHEMICAL FORMULA $CaSO_4$ • COLOR white, grayish, bluish, reddish, pale lavender • HARDNESS 3–3.5 • CLEAVAGE good, 3 directions at right angles • FRACTURE uneven • STREAK white to grayish • LUSTER glassy; pearly on 1 cleavage surface • OTHER transparent to translucent; sometimes fluorescent

Anhydrite is composed of calcium sulfate and is an important rock-forming mineral. It mainly occurs as a chemical precipitate in sedimentary rocks, where it is associated with the minerals halite and gypsum. It also occurs in openings near volcanoes. Its name comes from the Greek word *anhydrous*, which means "without water," emphasizing the mineral's lack of water molecules. Anhydrite may occur as fibrous masses (above) and rarely forms crystals (below).

→ LOOK FOR THIS

Anhydrite (below) is sometimes confused with gypsum because the two minerals often occur together and can have a similar appearance. However, gypsum is a softer mineral and doesn't have any cleavage faces that are at right angles to each other.

GLASSY LUSTER

10s spotters

RARELY FORMS CRYSTALS

GOOD CLEAVAGE; LIGHTWEIGHT

be a ROCK HOUND!

When water is added to anhydrite's chemical structure, the mineral changes to gypsum.

CHALCANTHITE

CHEMICAL FORMULA CuSO4 • 5H2O
- COLOR **deep blue, sky blue, greenish blue**
- HARDNESS **2.5** • CLEAVAGE **distinct**
- FRACTURE **rounded, like a scallop shell**
- STREAK **colorless to white** • LUSTER **glassy, dull** • OTHER **transparent to translucent; sometimes fluorescent**

Chalcanthite is a copper-sulfate mineral that contains water molecules. It can be easily recognized by its deep blue color, though some specimens are greenish. Crystals rarely form, but when they are present, they can be short and prismatic. Chalcanthite is a secondary mineral that forms as an alteration product of other copper minerals. It often occurs near Earth's surface in hydrothermal replacement deposits that are formed when rocks are dissolved by chemical processes. Chalcanthite is often found with the minerals aragonite and calcite.

CAN OCCUR AS MASSES EASILY DISSOLVED IN WATER

OFTEN DEEP BLUE

STALACTITE
Stalactites are icicle-like structures that hang from the ceilings of caves. They are formed from minerals deposited by water dripping from the ceiling. Chalcanthite stalactites form from copper-rich waters.

EXPERT'S CIRCLE

NAME GAME

The name "chalcanthite" comes from the Greek words *chalkos*, which means "copper," and *anthos*, which means "flower." It refers to the mineral's sometimes flowery appearance.

GLAUBERITE

CHEMICAL FORMULA $Na_2Ca(SO_4)_2$
- COLOR white, colorless, yellow, grayish; forms a white powdery coating when exposed to air • HARDNESS 2.5–3
- CLEAVAGE perfect, 1 direction • FRACTURE rounded, like a scallop shell • STREAK white • LUSTER glassy, greasy
- OTHER slightly salty taste

Glauberite is a sulfate mineral that contains calcium and sodium. It is a source of Glauber's salt, a chemical used to make paper, laundry detergent, and glass. Glauberite usually forms in and with salt beds deposited when saltwater lakes evaporate. It is associated with minerals such as halite and anhydrite. Under some conditions, glauberite goes through a process called dissolution: It dissolves then reforms as a different mineral, but in the same shape as the original glauberite.

SHAPES CAN INCLUDE PYRAMIDAL, PRISMATIC, AND TABLET.

be a ROCK HOUND!

Through dissolution, glauberite may be replaced by minerals like gypsum or calcite. This sometimes confuses mineral collectors, who think they have a glauberite specimen.

NO WELL-DEVELOPED CRYSTALS

COLORS INCLUDE BLUE AND YELLOWISH GREEN.

MELANTERITE

CHEMICAL FORMULA $FeSO_4 7H_2O$
- COLOR white, colorless, blue, yellowish green
- HARDNESS 2 • CLEAVAGE perfect, 1 direction
- FRACTURE rounded, like a scallop shell • STREAK white
- LUSTER glassy, dull • OTHER slightly sweet taste

Melanterite is a sulfate mineral that contains iron and water. It forms from the oxidation, or rusting, of iron sulfide minerals, such as pyrite and marcasite. Melanterite is usually white or colorless, but in some cases, the addition of copper can turn it green or even blue. This mineral rarely forms crystals. Instead, it can be found as masses covering other minerals or as stalactites hanging from cavities in a host rock.

ENARGITE

CHEMICAL FORMULA Cu_3AsS_4
- COLOR grayish black to iron black ○ HARDNESS 3
- CLEAVAGE perfect in 1 direction; distinct in 2 other directions ○ FRACTURE uneven, brittle ○ STREAK grayish black ○ LUSTER metallic; dull when tarnishes

Enargite is a type of sulfosalt—a group of minerals that have complicated structures. Enargite is an important ore of copper and can form tabular or prismatic crystals. Sometimes it occurs as masses or granular clusters. Enargite can often be found in hydrothermal veins with minerals such as galena, pyrite, and chalcopyrite.

BLACKISH COLOR; CRYSTALS PRISMATIC OR TABULAR

DISTINCT STRIATIONS ALONG THE CRYSTAL FACES

NAME GAME

Enargite gets its name from the Greek word *enargos,* which means "visible." The word refers to the mineral's distinct cleavage.

BOURNONITE

CHEMICAL FORMULA $PbCuSbS_3$
- COLOR steel gray to black ○ HARDNESS 2.5–3
- CLEAVAGE good in 1 direction; 2 others are fair and at right angles to the good cleavage face ○ FRACTURE somewhat rounded, like a scallop shell, to uneven ○ STREAK gray to black
- LUSTER metallic

Bournonite is a sulfosalt mineral that contains lead, copper, and an element called antimony. Bournonite is steel gray to black and often forms short, prismatic crystals that have smooth faces. Pairs of crystals called "twins" may sometimes appear in the shape of a cross. Bournonite usually occurs in hydrothermal veins with minerals such as galena, chalcopyrite, pyrite, and quartz.

APPEARS GRAY TO BLACK; VERY DENSE

NAME GAME

Because bournonite often forms cross-shaped twinned crystals, it has been unofficially named "cogwheel ore," because it looks like the gears found in many machines.

FLUORITE

CHEMICAL FORMULA CaF_2 • COLOR violet, blue, green, yellow, brown, bluish black, pink, rose red, colorless, white • HARDNESS 4 • CLEAVAGE perfect, 4 directions • FRACTURE uneven • STREAK white • LUSTER glassy

Fluorite is a mineral that's made of calcium and fluorine. It belongs to a group of minerals called halides, which contain one of the following elements: fluorine, chlorine, iodine, or bromine. Fluorite usually forms crystals that are cubic or twinned. It occurs in many different environments. This includes veins in Earth's crust, some metamorphic rocks, and deposits formed when rocks are dissolved by chemical processes.

BLUE JOHN

While fluorite is an industrial mineral used in the U.S. and around the world for smelting metal and making gasoline, it can also be beautiful to look at. Blue John is a type of fluorite that's characterized by bands of purple, blue, and yellow. It can be found in Blue John Cavern in Derbyshire, England.

EXPERT'S CIRCLE

PERFECT CLEAVAGE

CUBE- OR OCTAHEDRAL-SHAPED CRYSTALS

COLORS INCLUDE VIOLET, PINK, GREEN, AND YELLOW.

→ LOOK FOR THIS

Fluorite produces a blue color under ultraviolet light. This quality, called fluorescence, happens when fluorite absorbs the ultraviolet light and releases it as visible light of a different color. Many minerals are fluorescent under ultraviolet light, including calcite, willemite, and franklinite.

HALITE

CHEMICAL FORMULA NaCl
• COLOR colorless, white, gray, yellow, red, blue • HARDNESS 2–2.5 • CLEAVAGE perfect, 3 directions at right angles • FRACTURE rounded, like a scallop shell • STREAK white • LUSTER glassy

Halite is most often called rock salt, and it is one of the few minerals that people eat on purpose. When you sprinkle salt on your French fries, you are using tiny crystals of halite. Its name is derived from the Greek word *hals*, which means "salt." Halite usually forms cube-shaped crystals, but may also occur as "hoppers." These are cubic crystals in which the outer edges have grown faster than the centers, giving them a cavernous look. Halite typically forms as deposits that are left by evaporated seawater.

CRYOLITE

Cryolite is a white and colorless mineral that is similar in appearance to halite. However, cryolite is harder, and it can't easily dissolve in water as halite can.

EXPERT'S CIRCLE

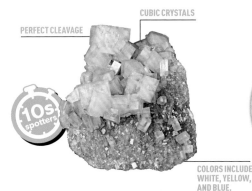

PERFECT CLEAVAGE

CUBIC CRYSTALS

10s spotters

COLORS INCLUDE WHITE, YELLOW, AND BLUE.

DIG THIS! Grab a magnifying glass, a shaker of table salt, and a piece of black construction paper. (Sea salt is better, since it has bigger crystals.) Sprinkle some salt on the paper, and study it through the magnifier. Can you see the cubic cleavage faces?

SYLVITE

CHEMICAL FORMULA **KCl**
- COLOR **colorless, white, gray, blue, pink**
- HARDNESS **2.5** • CLEAVAGE **perfect, 3 directions**
- FRACTURE **rounded** • STREAK **white** • LUSTER **glassy**
- OTHER **transparent, translucent**

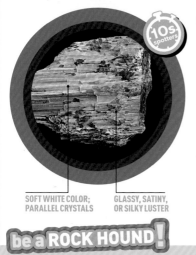

PERFECT CUBIC CLEAVAGE

INTERLOCKING CUBIC CRYSTALS

Sylvite is a halide mineral that contains potassium and chlorine and is similar to halite in that it forms cubic crystals that often interlock. Like halite, sylvite forms as deposits left by evaporated, mineral-rich seawater. Sylvite is a key source of the element potassium and is used in making fertilizers. It dissolves in water.

NAME GAME

"Sylvite" comes from the Latin phrase *sal digestivus Sylvii*, which means "digestive salt." It has been used as a salt substitute for people who cannot have the sodium in regular table salt.

ULEXITE

CHEMICAL FORMULA $NaCaB_5O_9 \cdot 8H_2O$
- COLOR **white** • HARDNESS **2.5** • CLEAVAGE **perfect in 1 direction; good in another** • FRACTURE **uneven, splintery** • STREAK **white** • LUSTER **glassy, satiny, silky**
- OTHER **transparent to translucent**

SOFT WHITE COLOR; PARALLEL CRYSTALS

GLASSY, SATINY, OR SILKY LUSTER

Ulexite is a major source of the element boron. Ulexite is usually found in rounded tufts that look like cotton balls. It occurs in the deposits of certain sedimentary rocks and is named after George Ludwig Ulex, the German chemist who determined the mineral's composition in 1850.

be a ROCK HOUND!

Ulexite can occur in parallel, sheetlike fibers, called television stone. The fibers act like light-transmitting cables: An image that appears on one surface of the mineral is transmitted to and can be seen on the opposite surface.

BORAX

CHEMICAL FORMULA $Na_2B_4O_7 \cdot 10H_2O$
- COLOR white, colorless, grayish to greenish white
- HARDNESS 2–2.5
- CLEAVAGE perfect in 1 direction; good in another
- FRACTURE rounded, like a scallop shell; brittle
- STREAK white
- LUSTER glassy, greasy

Borax is a borate mineral that forms in the evaporated deposits of saltwater lakes. It usually occurs with the minerals halite, ulexite, and kernite. Borax forms short, prismatic crystals and can be colorless, white, or gray. Although this mineral was first obtained from the salt lakes of Kashmir and Tibet, most borax today comes from the western United States.

PRISMATIC CRYSTALS DISSOLVE IN WATER.

SHORT, PRISMATIC CRYSTALS

COLORLESS, WHITE, OR GRAY

10s spotters

→ LOOK FOR THIS

Borax has many uses. When it is dissolved in water, it is used as a disinfectant and detergent booster. It is also used in ceramics, paint, glass, and coated paper. As you can see by the chemical formula, fresh borax contains water molecules (H_2O) in its crystal structure. After it has been exposed to air, however, the mineral's crystals dehydrate and become covered in a dull white coating. This coating is no longer pure borax, but another mineral called tincalconite. Tincalconite is common in the borax deposits of southern California, U.S.A., where it is mined today.

DIG THiS!

You can use borax—in the form of powdered soap—to make your own slime! Here's how:

- In a large plastic bowl, add 3/4 cup (175 mL) of warm water, 1 cup (250 mL) of white glue (that's an entire 8-ounce bottle), and 6 drops of food coloring in your favorite color. Stir the ingredients until they are well mixed.
- In a separate cup, add 2 teaspoons (5 mL) of Borax powder to a cup of warm water and stir. Then pour these ingredients into the glue mixture.
- Stir the ingredients for about 30 seconds or until they form a giant blob.

MONAZITE

CHEMICAL FORMULA $(Ce,La,Th,Nb)PO_4$
- COLOR yellow, yellowish brown, reddish brown
- HARDNESS 5–5.5 • CLEAVAGE distinct, sometimes parting in 1 direction • FRACTURE rounded, like a scallop shell; uneven
- STREAK white • LUSTER glassy, resinous (smooth)

SMALL GRAINS

REDDISH BROWN IN COLOR

Monazite belongs to a group of minerals called phosphates. It occurs as small grains within many types of igneous rocks, especially granite and pegmatite, and gneissic metamorphic rocks. Monazite is a resistant mineral that can withstand weathering and is often found in beach sands and soils. Monazite is also the name of a group of minerals that share some common traits in composition and crystal structure.

be a ROCK HOUND!

Some forms of monazite contain an element called cerium, which is used to polish glass, stone, and gemstones.

GREEN COLOR

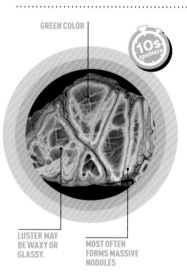

VARISCITE

CHEMICAL FORMULA $(Al,Fe)PO_4 • 2H_2O$
- COLOR pale green to emerald green, bluish green, colorless
- HARDNESS 4–4.5 • CLEAVAGE good in 1 direction; poor in second direction • FRACTURE uneven; splintery; rounded, like a scallop shell • STREAK white • LUSTER glassy, waxy

Variscite is a green phosphate mineral that occurs as fine-grained masses or tiny crystals. It's used as a gemstone and can be confused with turquoise—though turquoise is more blue. Variscite forms in cavities that were created when aluminum-bearing rocks were weathered by phosphate-rich waters. It occurs with apatite and limonite.

LUSTER MAY BE WAXY OR GLASSY.

MOST OFTEN FORMS MASSIVE NODULES

→ LOOK FOR THIS

Variscite is porous, meaning it has tiny spaces through which liquid or air can pass. So, when worn against the skin as jewelry, variscite tends to soak up body oils. This discolors the mineral.

AMBLYGONITE

CHEMICAL FORMULA $(Li,Na)Al(PO_4)(F,OH)$
· COLOR colorless, white, yellowish, beige, green, blue, gray · HARDNESS 5.5–6 · CLEAVAGE perfect in 1 direction; good in 3 others · FRACTURE uneven to somewhat rounded, like a scallop shell · STREAK white
· LUSTER glassy, greasy

Amblygonite is a phosphate mineral often found in pegmatite veins with other minerals, such as lepidolite, spodumene, and tourmaline. Sometimes it occurs in large masses embedded in quartz or feldspar. Amblygonite may form crystals that are short, prismatic, or tabular. At times they can be lath-shaped, which means they resemble the shape of a long, thin piece of wood.

USUALLY HAS A GLASSY OR GREASY LUSTER

COLORS INCLUDE WHITE, YELLOW, BEIGE, AND BLUE.

LATH-SHAPED CRYSTALS HELP IDENTIFY AMBLYGONITE.

NAME GAME

Amblygonite gets its name from the Greek word *amblygonios,* which means "blunt angles." The name is a reference to the mineral's cleavage.

OLIVENITE

CHEMICAL FORMULA Cu_2AsO_4OH
· COLOR olive green, greenish brown, brown, yellowish
· HARDNESS 3 · CLEAVAGE poor, 2 directions · FRACTURE rounded, like a scallop shell, to irregular · STREAK colorless
· LUSTER somewhat brilliant to glassy

Olivenite is a greenish mineral that contains copper and arsenic. It may form different crystal shapes, including long or short prisms, globs, or kidney shapes with a fibrous structure. Olivenite occurs in deposits formed in rocks that have been altered by chemical processes and can be found with minerals such as malachite, azurite, and limonite.

USUALLY MASSIVE, AND MAY FORM GLOBULAR NODULES

WILL DISSOLVE IN HYDROCHLORIC ACID

GREENISH COLOR

NAME GAME

The name "olivenite" comes from the German word *olivenerz,* which means "olive ore." It refers to the green color.

APATITE

CHEMICAL FORMULA $Ca_5(PO_4)_3(F,OH,Cl)$

- **COLOR** green, brown, red, yellow, violet, pink, white
- **HARDNESS** 5 • **CLEAVAGE** poor, 1 direction crosswise
- **FRACTURE** uneven; rounded, like a scallop shell
- **STREAK** white • **LUSTER** glassy, greasy
- **OTHER** transparent to translucent

The name "apatite" is used to describe a group of phosphate minerals that vary in color, but have a similar crystal structure. They are the most common minerals containing phosphate and are used in the making of phosphate fertilizers. The crystals are short or long prisms with hexagonal faces. They're also tabular (shaped like a tablet). Apatite may occur in masses or as small, irregular lumps called nodules. Apatite minerals can be found in many intrusive igneous as well as some metamorphic rocks.

FLUORAPATITE

Fluorapatite is the most common mineral in the apatite group. It is colorless or white when pure, but can also occur in blues, greens, yellow, red, and violet. Fluorapatite can be found in igneous rocks, such as granite pegmatite and syenite, and in calcium-bearing metamorphic rocks.

EXPERT'S CIRCLE

PRISMATIC CRYSTALS WITH HEXAGONAL FACES

10s spotters

GREASY OR GLASSY LUSTER

NAME GAME

"Apatite" comes from the Greek term *apate*, meaning "deceit." The minerals in the apatite group got this name because some of them look like other popular minerals, including aquamarine, amethyst, and olivenite.

PYROMORPHITE

CHEMICAL FORMULA $Pb_5(PO_4)_3Cl$
- COLOR green, yellow, brown, white, gray
- HARDNESS 3.5-4 • CLEAVAGE none • FRACTURE somewhat rounded, like a scallop shell; uneven • STREAK pale yellow, white, or greenish yellow • LUSTER resinous, greasy, brilliant

Pyromorphite is a member of the phosphate group, and it is a minor ore of lead. It forms as a secondary mineral due to the chemical alteration of other minerals that contain lead and can often be found with galena and vanadinite. Its colors include green, brown, and yellow. Pyromorphite crystals can be hexagon-shaped prisms, barrel-shaped, or cavernous.

CRYSTALS CAN BE CAVERNOUS, BARREL-SHAPED, OR PRISMATIC.

MINERAL OFTEN HAS A RESINOUS, OR HONEYLIKE, LUSTER.

NAME GAME

Because it quickly crystalizes after being melted, pyromorphite gets its name from the Greek words *pyr,* which means "fire," and *morphe,* which means "form."

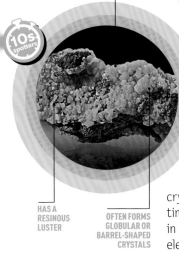

FOUND IN LEAD DEPOSITS

HAS A RESINOUS LUSTER

OFTEN FORMS GLOBULAR OR BARREL-SHAPED CRYSTALS

MIMETITE

CHEMICAL FORMULA $Pb_5(AsO_4)_3Cl$
- COLOR yellow, orange, brown, green • HARDNESS 3.5-4
- CLEAVAGE poor • FRACTURE somewhat rounded, like a scallop shell, to uneven • STREAK nearly white • LUSTER resinous

Mimetite belongs to a group of minerals called arsenates and is similar to pyromorphite, except it contains arsenic instead of phosphorus. It is a secondary mineral and a minor ore of lead, forming as a result of the alteration of other lead minerals. Its crystals form globular, needlelike, and sometimes tabular shapes. Mimetite can be found in some lead deposits and in areas where the elements lead and arsenic occur together.

VANADINITE

CHEMICAL FORMULA $Pb_3(VO_4)_3Cl$
- COLOR red, orange, brown, yellow, multicolored
- HARDNESS 3 ◦ CLEAVAGE none ◦ FRACTURE rounded, like a scallop shell; uneven ◦ STREAK white, pale yellow ◦ LUSTER brilliant, resinous ◦ OTHER transparent to translucent

Vanadinite is a rare mineral. Like mimetite and pyromorphite, it contains lead. Since lead is a weighty element, it makes vanadinite heavy as well. The mineral may occur in several colors, but bright red and orange are the most popular among collectors. Vanadinite can be found in lead deposits associated with minerals such as galena, goethite, narite, and wulfenite.

SHORT CRYSTALS ARE HEXAGONAL PRISMS. EACH PRISM HAS TWO HEXAGON-SHAPED BASES AND SIX RECTANGULAR SIDES.

be a ROCK HOUND!

Vanadinite usually forms short crystals. But specimens from a mine in Namibia have crystals more than 4.7 inches (12 cm) long.

WAVELLITE

CHEMICAL FORMULA $Al_3(PO_4)_2(OH)_3 \cdot 5H_2O$
- COLOR green, yellow, white, gray, brown ◦ HARDNESS 3.5–4
- CLEAVAGE perfect in 1 direction; good in 2 directions
- FRACTURE rounded, like a scallop shell; uneven ◦ STREAK white
- LUSTER glassy, pearly ◦ OTHER transparent to translucent

Wavellite is an aluminum-phosphate mineral with a striking appearance. Clusters of small, needlelike crystals fan out to form structures that resemble flowers. The crystals are usually green and sometimes exhibit uneven coloring that results from impurities. Wavellite can usually be found in some metamorphic rocks and near veins in igneous rocks.

USUALLY GREEN IN COLOR

CLUSTERS OF NEEDLELIKE CRYSTALS RADIATE, OR FAN OUT, FROM A CENTRAL POINT.

NAME GAME

Wavellite was discovered in 1785, but wasn't analyzed until 30 years later by mineralogist William Wavell. The mineral is named after him.

TURQUOISE

CHEMICAL FORMULA $CuAl_6(PO_4)_4OH_8 \cdot 4-5H_2O$
- **COLOR** sky blue, bluish green, apple green
- **HARDNESS** 5–6 • **CLEAVAGE** none • **FRACTURE** rounded, like a scallop shell • **STREAK** white, pale green
- **LUSTER** waxy, dull • **OTHER** somewhat translucent to opaque

Turquoise is a blue phosphate mineral that's been a popular gemstone for thousands of years. Cultures ranging from ancient Egyptians to modern-day Navajo have used the mineral in decorative ways. Turquoise typically forms in dry regions when rain trickles down through soil and rock and dissolves copper. When the rainwater eventually evaporates, copper combines with two other elements—phosphorus and aluminum—to form small amounts of turquoise.

GLASSY LUSTER

BRIGHT BLUE-GREEN COLOR

FAUSTITE

"Turquoise" isn't just the name of a single mineral, it's also the name of a group of minerals that share a similar chemical composition. Faustite is a bright-green member of the group that can be found in some parts of the U.S. states of Colorado, Nevada, and Utah. Faustite is nearly identical to turquoise, except that it contains zinc in place of copper.

EXPERT'S CIRCLE

be a ROCK HOUND!

The Aztecs created death masks, which they placed over the faces of the dead. Some masks were ornate and decorated with turquoise mosaic.

AUTUNITE

CHEMICAL FORMULA $Ca(UO_2)_2(PO_4)_2 \cdot 10-12H_2O$
- COLOR **lemon yellow to lime green**
- HARDNESS **2-2.5** • CLEAVAGE **perfect, 1 direction**
- FRACTURE **flakes** • STREAK **yellowish** • LUSTER **pearly, somewhat brilliant** • OTHER **transparent to translucent; very fluorescent**

Autunite is a very fluorescent phosphate mineral that glows bright green under ultraviolet light. The mineral's fluorescence is caused largely by the presence of uranium, a radioactive element, in its chemical composition. Autunite is a secondary mineral and occurs in some granite pegmatites and in veins, or fractures, and is an alteration product of other uranium-rich minerals.

FLAT, TABULAR CRYSTALS

LEMON YELLOW OR LIME GREEN COLOR

⚠ DANGER!

Since autunite is radioactive, you should always take extreme care in handling this mineral. Wear gloves when handling this mineral, and never taste it or inhale dust that occurs after breaking it.

FLUORESCENT, SOFT, AND DENSE, SO IT FEELS SLIGHTLY HEAVY; FORMS PYRAMID-SHAPED CRYSTALS

→ LOOK FOR THIS
Scheelite is a major source of the metal tungsten, which is used to make lighting filaments, wires, sheets, and rods.

SCHEELITE

CHEMICAL FORMULA $CaWO_4$
- COLOR **white, colorless, gray, yellowish orange, brownish, greenish** • HARDNESS **4.5-5** • CLEAVAGE **distinct in 1 direction; poor in 2 directions** • FRACTURE **rounded, like a scallop shell; uneven** • STREAK **white to yellowish** • LUSTER **glassy, brilliant**
- OTHER **transparent to translucent; very fluorescent**

Scheelite is a mineral rich in the element tungsten and is strongly fluorescent. Although the mineral usually appears orange to brown in natural light, it produces a bright-blue glow under ultraviolet light. Scheelite usually forms crystals that resemble octahedrons and occurs mostly in metamorphic rocks, but can also be found in some veins and pegmatites.

WULFENITE

CHEMICAL FORMULA $PbMoO_4$
- COLOR yellow, orange, brown, yellowish gray, whitish • HARDNESS 3 • CLEAVAGE distinct, 1 direction
- FRACTURE somewhat rounded, like a scallop shell; uneven • STREAK white • LUSTER greasy to resinous
- OTHER transparent to translucent

Wulfenite is a mineral that contains lead and molybdenum, a metallic element that's used to strengthen steel. Wulfenite occurs in brilliant colors that range from yellow to brown and forms as either thin plates or square, tabular crystals. Wulfenite is a secondary mineral that occurs with lead and molybdenum deposits and can be found with minerals such as molybdenite, barite, and calcite.

GREASY LUSTER

BRIGHT COLORS, SUCH AS YELLOW, ORANGE, BROWN, AND WHITE

THIN PLATES OR SQUARE, TABULAR CRYSTALS

NAME GAME

Wulfenite is named after Franz Xaver Wulfen, an Austrian mineralogist.

AMBER

CHEMICAL FORMULA C, H, O
- COLOR golden yellow to golden orange
- HARDNESS 2–2.5 • CLEAVAGE none • FRACTURE rounded, like a scallop shell • STREAK white • LUSTER resinous
- OTHER transparent to translucent

Technically, amber is not a mineral because it's a product of a living thing. Amber started as a sticky substance called tree sap resin that oozed out of cone-bearing trees and hardened over time to form what we call amber today. Amber can be found in the United States in California, New Jersey, and Kansas. It's also found around the world and is most common along the shores of the Baltic Sea.

TRANSLUCENT

LUSTER IS RESINOUS

HAS A GOLDEN YELLOW OR ORANGE COLOR

be a ROCK HOUND!

Some ancient insects got caught in tree resin, and their remains became preserved in the hardened substance. In 2013, scientists identified a 230-million-year-old mite in this piece of amber.

ALL ABOUT ROCKS

By now, you know that most rocks are made of different minerals. Some rocks have many minerals in them; others have just a few. In some cases, rocks do not contain minerals, but instead are made from natural materials produced by living things!

Scientists study these different ingredients to help identify specific rocks—and to learn how they formed. Why is this important? Tracing a rock's origin can give us valuable information about Earth's past. For example, it may tell us if a volcano or a lake once existed in the area where the rock was found. Or, it may reveal how a mountain range formed. In addition to the parts or ingredients of a rock, scientists also study the shape and arrangement of the minerals that give rocks their patterns and textures.

After scientists have figured out how a rock formed, they place it in one of three groups: igneous, metamorphic, or sedimentary. Read on to learn more.

Igneous

Igneous rocks form when magma—a hot molten rock found deep inside Earth—cools and hardens into rock in interlocking grains, like pieces of a puzzle. Sometimes the magma hardens inside Earth to form intrusive-igneous rocks like the granite below. Other times it flows up to Earth's surface and erupts from a volcano. When this happens, the magma is called lava. The lava then cools and hardens into volcanic igneous rock like the obsidian below.

OBSIDIAN

GRANITE

GNEISS

Metamorphic

Metamorphic rocks, like gneiss and marble, left, are rocks that have been changed from their original form. This change occurs when the rocks are heated and/or squeezed in Earth's crust. The rocks may by heated by magma flowing through the rocks, or they may be squeezed when mountains are built. This intense heat or pressure may cause the structure—and often the composition—of the rock to change and become another rock. This change that the rock goes through is called metamorphism.

LIMESTONE

MARBLE

Sedimentary

Sedimentary rocks are also formed by changes that occur to other rocks. But unlike metamorphic rocks, these changes occur near Earth's surface. Sometimes water, wind, and ice are responsible for the changes. These forces wear away a rock, producing small particles called sediment. Over time, these particles accumulate in layers and harden into rock. These are called sedimentary clastic, like conglomerate, below. Other sedimentary rocks are the result of chemical changes and are called sedimentary chemical, like limestone, right. This occurs when mineral-rich water evaporates and ultimately forms crystals.

CONGLOMERATE

Rock Vitals

A block of vital information starts each rock entry. The term "grain size" refers to the size of the grains that make up sedimentary clastic rocks, and it also refers to the size of the crystals that make up igneous, metamorphic, and sedimentary chemical rocks. Each entry gives the major and minor minerals present in the rock. For instance, quartzite rock contains a lot of the mineral quartz and a little of the mineral sillimanite. Finally, the term "texture" tells you whether the rock is rough, layered, has cavities, and more. For sedimentary clastic rocks, you'll find the terms "organic matter" and "structure," which tell what once-living matter is in the rock and where it's found in nature.

HOW WE USE ROCKS

From carving tools to building stones, rocks have played an important role in human history.

Tools

More than two million years ago, humans didn't have sophisticated tools. So, they learned to use rocks to perform everyday tasks, such as cutting, chopping, and hunting with arrowheads. This early period is often called the Stone Age. In some cultures, stone tools are still being used today.

QUARTZITE

During the Stone Age, hard stones, such as quartzite, above, were used to strike and shape softer rocks into useful objects. This included hammers, nut grinders, and scraping tools.

Art

LASCAUX CAVES

Early humans found that rocks could be used in creative ways. They ground up minerals, such as hematite, and used them to paint pictures on rock walls. They also carved images into rocks—often with tools made from rocks.

In the early 1940s, two teenagers discovered a series of caves in southwestern France. The Lascaux Caves, as they are now known, had paintings of animals on the walls, left. Experts estimate that the paintings are about 17,300 years old.

People also made sculptures, such as Venus figurines, which resemble a heavy or pregnant woman. These Venuses were created by artists in Paleolithic cultures across Europe. Dating from between 33,000 to 20,000 B.C.E., the figurines have been unearthed at different sites. Many were sculpted from soft sedimentary rocks like limestone, while others are carved from bone or wood.

LINCOLN MEMORIAL

Rock art has become much more sophisticated over the years. This statue of Abraham Lincoln, right, which sits in the Lincoln Memorial in Washington, D.C., U.S.A., was carved from Georgia marble, a metamorphic rock.

PETRA

Buildings

Over time, people discovered that rocks could be used to build structures, such as homes, temples, and tombs. Some cultures excavated, or carved out, rock to make these structures. Others used cut stones.

Petra, located in Jordan, is a city carved into sandstone cliffs. It dates back to around 300 B.C.E. and was occupied until about 363 C.E. by an ancient Arab people called the Nabataeans.

CAPPADOCIA, TURKEY

Ancient volcanic eruptions covered what is now Cappadocia, Turkey, right, in ash. This ash hardened into a soft rock called tuff. Natural weathering turned the landscape into a series of towers and spires, which people chiseled into homes.

The Taj Mahal is a mausoleum, or tomb, in India that's built with white marble called Makrana, named after a town in India. The building was commissioned by the Mughal emperor Shah Jahan to honor his late wife. It took more than 22,000 workers 22 years to build the Taj Mahal. It was completed in 1653.

TAJ MAHAL

THE ROCK CYCLE

2 Some of the magma remains in place. Eventually, it cools and hardens into igneous rocks, such as granite or diorite. The magma that doesn't remain in place rises to Earth's surface. There, it can be erupted as lava from a volcano. As the lava cools, it hardens into igneous volcanic rock such as basalt.

For billions of years, rocks have gone through a type of recycling process called the rock cycle. During this process, one type of rock is transformed into another. For example, under certain conditions, an igneous rock can become a sedimentary rock. After much time, that sedimentary rock can alter, or change, into a metamorphic rock.

When Earth first formed, all of the rocks formed from melted material. After that time, the rock cycle began changing the rocks on the planet. For a better idea of how it works, check out the diagram at right. The words with colored numbers relate to the arrows and explain what's going on at each step.

cooling

magma

1 Deep underground, metamorphic rocks melt to form molten rock called magma.

melting

Metamorphic Rock

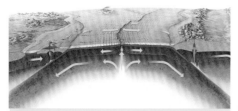

5 The upper portion of Earth's mantle and crust is broken up into huge slabs of moving rock called tectonic plates. Some plates spread apart and release magma, while others collide. When that happens, rocks on the surface can be pushed back under the surface, where they are heated and/or squeezed. Eventually, they form metamorphic rocks.

Igneous Rock

melting

heat and
pressure

3 Rocks on Earth's surface are battered by rain, wind, and ice. Over time, these forces of nature dissolve the rocks and break them into small particles. This process is called weathering. Erosion occurs when forces of nature like streams, wind, and glaciers move the weathered particles downhill. Eventually, the particles are deposited as sediments into streams, lakes, and oceans.

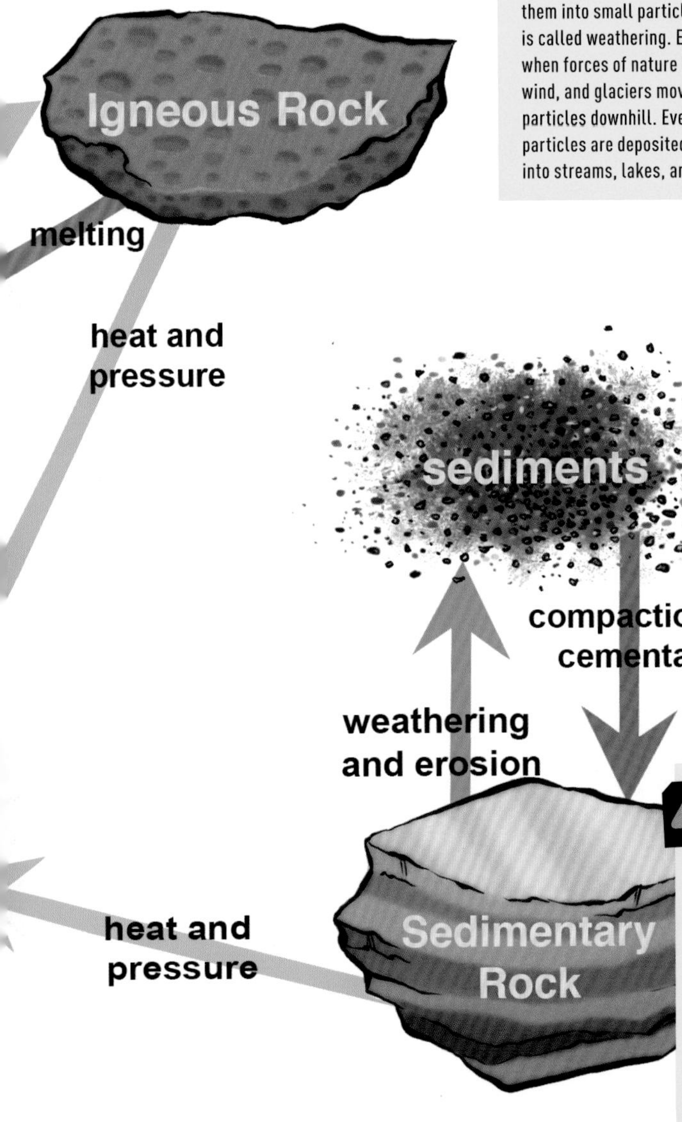

sediments

compaction and
cementation

weathering
and erosion

4 The loose sediments are squeezed and cemented together to form sedimentary rock. Over time, it either weathers and returns to sediment or is driven back under Earth's surface through plate tectonics.

heat and
pressure

**Sedimentary
Rock**

BASALT

- **COLOR** dark gray to black • **GRAIN SIZE** less than 0.1 mm
- **MAJOR MINERALS** sodium plagioclase, pyroxene, olivine
- **MINOR MINERALS** leucite, nepheline, augite
- **TEXTURE** may be pitted with many cavities called vesicles

Basalt is the most common rock on Earth's surface. Most of the ocean floor is made of basalt. The rock can also be found on many landmasses, particularly Ireland, Iceland, the western United States, and Hawaii. Basalt is a dark, fine-grained igneous rock. It forms when magma that's rich in magnesium and iron is erupted by volcanoes. The magma—called lava when it reaches Earth's surface—cools quickly and hardens to form basalt. It forms a pillow shape if the lava is erupted from an underwater volcano.

→ LOOK FOR THIS

Basalt is sometimes confused with andesite, below, another igneous-volcanic rock. The difference is that basalt forms at a more shallow depth than andesite. Therefore, it cools more quickly and doesn't have time to form large crystals. This makes the rock fine -grained. Andesite cools at a slower rate, which allows some larger crystals to form. As a result, andesite can have some visible crystals.

DARK-COLORED

FINE CRYSTALS, NOT USUALLY VISIBLE TO NAKED EYE

10s spotters

RHYOLITE

- COLOR light to medium gray, light pink
- GRAIN SIZE less than 0.1 mm
- MAJOR MINERALS quartz, potassium feldspar
- MINOR MINERALS biotite, amphibole, plagioclase, pyroxene • TEXTURE has bands; sometimes the bands have a glassy texture and small cavities

Rhyolite is a light-colored igneous rock with small crystals. It forms when magma that's rich in silica is erupted from a volcano. Once on Earth's surface, the magma—now in lava form—cools quickly and hardens into rhyolite. This cooling process is so rapid that crystals don't have much time to form. The crystals are thus very tiny and may give the rock a glassy appearance.

MOST CRYSTALS TOO SMALL TO BE SEEN BY THE NAKED EYE

SOME HAVE A MIXTURE OF GRAIN SIZES, INCLUDING GLASSY PIECES.

LIGHT-COLORED

be a ROCK HOUND!

Rhyolite magma is very viscous, meaning that it flows very slowly. When gas bubbles form in viscous magma, they are unable to escape. This leads to explosive volcanic eruptions.

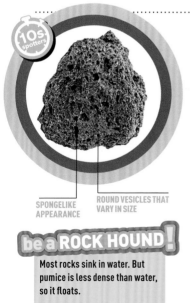

SPONGELIKE APPEARANCE

ROUND VESICLES THAT VARY IN SIZE

be a ROCK HOUND!

Most rocks sink in water. But pumice is less dense than water, so it floats.

PUMICE

- COLOR black, white, yellow, brown
- GRAIN SIZE less than 0.1 mm • MAJOR MINERAL glass
- MINOR MINERALS feldspar, augite, hornblende, zircon
- TEXTURE numerous cavities, cavities that vary in size

Pumice is an igneous-volcanic rock that forms from magma that's full of gases and water. During a volcanic eruption, this magma produces frothy lava. As the lava cools and hardens, the gas bubbles become trapped. The result is a rock with many vesicles, or cavities, that vary in size. And it's lightweight. Pumice is considered a volcanic glass because the lava that forms the rock undergoes such a rapid cooling process that crystals can't form.

TUFF

- **COLOR** light to dark brown • **GRAIN SIZE** 0.1 mm–2 mm
- **MAJOR MINERALS** glassy fragments
- **MINOR MINERALS** crystal fragments
- **TEXTURE** can show signs of bedding, which occurs when volcanic debris falls back to Earth and settles in layers

SOFT; CAN OCCUR IN LAYERS

FRAGMENTS OF ROCK AND ASH MAY BE VISIBLE.

Tuff is an igneous rock that results from an explosive volcanic eruption. When the volcano erupts, it blasts hot ash, rock fragments, and magma into the air. When this debris falls back to Earth, it is sometimes cemented together into rock. This rock is known as tuff. Tuff is found in the area around a volcano's vent, or opening. The closer the tuff is to the vent, the larger and thicker it is. Tuff is generally a soft rock and can occur in layers. Each layer represents a different volcanic blast.

be a ROCK HOUND!

Easter Island, in the Pacific Ocean, has hundreds of mysterious stone statues in human shapes. Most are made from tuff, while others are carved from basalt, scoria, and trachyte.

TRACHYTE

FINE-GRAINED; ROUGH TEXTURE

- **COLOR** off-white, gray, pale yellow, pink
- **GRAIN SIZE** less than 0.1 mm • **MAJOR MINERALS** sanidine, oligoclase
- **MINOR MINERALS** feldspathoids, quartz, hornblende, pyroxene, biotite
- **TEXTURE** streaked or banded

OFTEN LARGE CRYSTALS; SOMETIMES STREAKS OR BANDS

Trachyte is a fine-grained igneous-volcanic rock with a rough texture. It is composed mainly of feldspar minerals—usually sanidine. The sanidine occurs as tabular, or tablet-shaped, crystals that are packed tightly together in a parallel manner. This arrangement, which is caused by the flow of lava as it cools, gives the rock a banded appearance. In many samples, larger crystals called phenocrysts are also common—often of a darker mineral. Trachyte gets its name from the Greek term *trachos*, which means "rough."

DACITE

- COLOR gray to pink • GRAIN SIZE less than 0.1 mm
- MAJOR MINERALS quartz, plagioclase
- MINOR MINERALS leucite, biotite, hornblende, pyroxene
- TEXTURE fine-grained mass with some larger crystals

Dacite, a volcanic rock often found along the edges of continents, forms from lava that is fairly rich in silica. The lava from which dacite forms is usually viscous, or sticky, and often produces round structures called domes along the edge of volcanoes. On the surface, dacite will frequently have flowlike structures. In many cases, it also has larger crystals called phenocrysts, which have become trapped in the lava in the finer-grained rock.

FINE TO MEDIUM GRAINS

OFTEN HAS VISIBLE QUARTZ AND/OR PLAGIOCLASE CRYSTALS

USUALLY LIGHT GRAY

be a ROCK HOUND!

Like rhyolite, dacite lava is viscous and can be explosive. In 1980, a dacite dome may have caused the eruption of Mount St. Helens, in the U.S. state of Washington.

FINE-TO-MEDIUM–GRAINED

PHENOCRYSTS OF PLAGIOCLASE OR PYROXENE OFTEN VISIBLE

ANDESITE

- COLOR light to dark gray, reddish pink
- GRAIN SIZE less than 0.1 mm
- MAJOR MINERALS plagioclase feldspars
- MINOR MINERALS pyroxene, amphibole, biotite
- TEXTURE fine-grained mass, with some large crystals

Andesite is an igneous-volcanic rock. It forms from lava that has a relatively low silica content and is often erupted from a stratovolcano. This is a type of cone-shaped volcano made of alternating layers of ash, lava, and cinders. Some andesite stratovolcanoes include Mount Shasta, Mount Hood, and Mount Adams in the United States and Mount Fuji in Japan.

NAME GAME

Andesite rock is named after the Andes, a mountain range in South America. In addition to forming in lava flows, andesite can also form dikes, which cut across other rock types near the surface.

SCORIA

- COLOR dark brown, reddish brown, or black
- GRAIN SIZE less than 0.1 mm
- MAJOR MINERALS plagioclase, pyroxene
- MINOR MINERALS olivine, biotite, hornblende, magnetite
- TEXTURE many holes (vesicles) filled in with crystals

SMALL, ROUNDED HOLES, OR VESICLES

USUALLY A DARK COLOR

Scoria is a dark igneous rock similar to pumice but not as lightweight. It forms from magma that's filled with dissolved gas. When lava exits the volcano, this dissolved gas begins to escape in the form of bubbles. If the bubbles don't escape by the time the lava hardens, they are trapped inside. The result is a rock filled with many small, rounded holes called vesicles. Scoria usually accumulates near the vents of cone-shaped volcanoes.

NAME GAME

Some people describe small pieces of scoria as cinder found in a coal oven. This has earned scoria the nickname "cinders." In fact, many of the volcanoes that they form in and erupt from are known as "cinder cones."

OBSIDIAN

- COLOR black, red, brown
- GRAIN SIZE none
- MAJOR MINERAL glass
- MINOR MINERALS hematite, feldspar
- TEXTURE can exhibit streaks or bands that result from flowing lava; fracture is rounded, like a scallop shell

USUALLY BLACK; GLASSY LUSTER

FRACTURE ROUNDED LIKE A SCALLOP SHELL

Obsidian is a glassy igneous rock that is usually black, dark brown, or red in color and found near volcanoes. It forms from the same magma as rhyolite. The main difference between the two is that rhyolite is a crystallized rock, while obsidian is a volcanic glass. This means that it cools too quickly to form crystals. When obsidian is broken, it can produce fragments with sharp edges. For this reason, obsidian was used as knives and spear points up to the 20th century and is still used in some cultures to make ceremonial weapons. Ancient people in what is now Mexico polished obsidian for mirrors.

GRANITE

- COLOR **white, light gray, pink, red**
- GRAIN SIZE **2–5 mm** • MAJOR MINERALS **potassium feldspar, plagioclase feldspar, quartz**
- MINOR MINERALS **muscovite, biotite, hornblende**
- TEXTURE **coarse grains; large crystals possible**

Granite is the most common igneous rock in Earth's continental crust. It is light-colored and has large crystals. Like other intrusive-igneous rocks, it forms when magma slowly cools and hardens into a solid beneath Earth's surface. Because the cooling process is slow, the minerals that make up the rock are able to form larger crystals than they would at Earth's surface, where the cooling process is quicker. Granite becomes exposed on Earth's surface when overlying material is worn away over millions of years. It is often found forming mountains in areas where the surrounding softer rock has worn away.

10s spotters

LIGHT-COLORED ROCK

LARGE CRYSTALS OF QUARTZ, FELDSPARS, SOMETIMES MICAS

PINK GRANITE

The type of minerals that are present in granite can affect the color of the rock. In the case of pink granite, the color likely comes from the presence of orthoclase, a pink feldspar.

EXPERT'S CIRCLE

be a ROCK HOUND!

Granite kitchen countertops and tiles are common. Granite sculptures include Mount Rushmore National Memorial in the Black Hills, South Dakota, U.S.A. (top) and simple garden ornaments (right).

GRANITE PEGMATITE

- COLOR can vary greatly, depending on the minerals present
- GRAIN SIZE at least 1.0 cm • MAJOR MINERALS quartz, feldspar, mica
- MINOR MINERALS apatite, lepidolite, monazite, topaz, tourmaline, to name a few • TEXTURE very large crystals

Granite pegmatite is an intrusive-igneous rock that's similar to granite in composition. Both rocks contain quartz, feldspar, and mica. However, granite pegmatite contains much larger crystals. The reason for the large crystals is that pegmatite magmas usually have a great deal of water in them. This allows the atoms that form the crystals to move quickly and build on each other. A mass of granite pegmatite may have tablet-like, podlike, or sheetlike shapes.

LARGE CRYSTALS AVERAGE 1 INCH (2.5 CM) ACROSS

OFTEN TABLET-LIKE OR SHEETLIKE SHAPE

be a ROCK HOUND!

Granite pegmatite crystals can be 33 feet (10 m) across—longer than a limousine!

OCCURS IN DIKES

SYENITE

- COLOR gray, pink, red, • GRAIN SIZE 2–5 mm • MAJOR MINERAL feldspar • MINOR MINERALS plagioclase, biotite, amphibole, pyroxene, hornblende, and feldspathoids such as sodalite
- TEXTURE medium-to-coarse crystals

Syenite is an intrusive-igneous rock similar to granite but composed mainly of feldspar, with little or no quartz. Other minerals may also be present, including biotite or hornblende. Syenite is often formed from magma that's made of partly molten granite and is found along the edges of larger masses of granite. It can occur as a dike—a long, thin mass of rock that forms in the fracture of another rock.

SIMILAR TO GRANITE, EXCEPT THAT IT HAS LITTLE OR NO QUARTZ

→ LOOK FOR THIS
Some varieties of syenite are blue because they contain the mineral sodalite. These blue varieties are sometimes used as decorative stones.

DIORITE

- COLOR black or dark green, mottled with gray or white
- GRAIN SIZE 2–5 mm • MAJOR MINERALS plagioclase, hornblende
- MINOR MINERAL biotite • TEXTURE medium-to-coarse crystals

Diorite is a coarse-grained, intrusive-igneous rock with large crystals. It forms from magma that cools beneath Earth's surface. Diorite magma can flow horizontally into any cracks or spaces in other rocks, forming a flat layer of rock called a sill. It may also be found as a dike—a thin strip of rock formed in the fracture of another rock. It has a salt-and-pepper appearance because it's made of the light-colored mineral plagioclase and some dark-colored minerals, such as hornblende or biotite.

SALT-AND-PEPPER LOOK

LIGHT-COLORED PLAGIOCLASE AND DARK-COLORED MINERALS

→ LOOK FOR THIS

Diorite has decorative uses. Look for it in some museum sculptures.

MONZONITE

- COLOR light to medium gray; sometimes pink, dark gray, or greenish gray • GRAIN SIZE 0.5–2 cm
- MAJOR MINERALS feldspar (such as orthoclase), hornblende, augite, biotite • MINOR MINERALS apatite, magnetite, ilmenite, titanite, quartz
- TEXTURE medium-size grains

MAY APPEAR SLIGHTLY PINK WHEN ORTHOCLASE IS PRESENT

USUALLY LIGHT TO MEDIUM GRAY

Monzonite is an intrusive-igneous rock that forms when magma cools slowly beneath Earth's surface. It often occurs in small masses—usually along the border of larger rock masses such as diorite. Monzonite's composition is similar to granite's, except that it contains much less quartz and more plagioclase feldspar.

be a ROCK HOUND!

When more than 10 percent of monzonite is made of quartz, it's called quartz monzonite. It was used to build the Salt Lake Temple in Utah, U.S.A.

ROCK STARS: Fossils

SHELLS

Many fossils aren't actually the shells of organisms that died. Rather, they are copies that formed after the shell was buried in sediment. The soft parts of the body rot away quickly, while the hard parts remain. The shell is covered by sediment, which turns into rock. Eventually, the rock is worn away, leaving the shell fossil behind.

Fossils

When most people hear the word "fossil," they think of dinosaurs. But a fossil can be the remains of any living thing that has been preserved over time. This includes plants, insects, and even bacteria. Not all organisms become fossils when they die. That's because they decay too quickly to be preserved. However, an insect covered with resin, a sticky substance produced by plants, can be fossilized. Other fossils are found mainly in sedimentary rocks.

POOP

Not all fossils are the skeletal remains of an organism. In 1998, a giant coprolite, or fossilized poop, was discovered in sedimentary rock in Saskatchewan, Canada! The coprolite was 17 inches (43 cm) long and 6 inches (15 m) thick. Scientists believe it was deposited by a *Tyrannosaurus rex*.

PLANTS

In some fossil beds of sedimentary rock, imprints of leaves, fern fronds, seed cones, and even bark are so perfectly preserved that minute details are visible through microscopes. The heat and pressure acting on a plant can leave a detailed carbon impression of it in sedimentary rock.

INSECTS

The insect in this rock was covered by plant resin millions of years ago. When the sap hardened, it formed a rock called amber, with a perfectly preserved animal inside.

GABBRO

- **COLOR** dark gray to black • **GRAIN SIZE** 2–5 mm • **MAJOR MINERALS** calcium plagioclase feldspar, pyroxene, ilmenite • **MINOR MINERALS** olivine, magnetite • **TEXTURE** medium-to-coarse crystals

Gabbro is a medium-to-coarse–grained intrusive-igneous rock. It forms from the same magma as basalt. But basalt is erupted from a volcano and so cools quickly above-ground, whereas gabbro cools slowly inside Earth. The slow cooling makes larger crystals.

LARGE CRYSTALS; COARSE GRAINS

ROCK MAY BE SHEETLIKE OR SAUCER-SHAPED.

DIABASE

- **COLOR** dark gray to black • **GRAIN SIZE** 1–2 mm
- **MAJOR MINERAL** plagioclase feldspar • **MINOR MINERALS** pyroxene, hornblende, olivine, magnetite • **TEXTURE** crystals generally less than 2 mm

Diabase, also called dolerite, is an intrusive-igneous rock formed from the same type of magma as gabbro. But it comes from the magma that moves toward Earth's surface and cools more quickly. This gives diabase smaller crystals than gabbro.

USUALLY OCCURS AS DIKES OR SILLS

HARD TO BREAK WITH A HAMMER; CRYSTALS USUAL-LY VISIBLE TO THE NAKED EYE, BUT OFTEN LESS THAN 2 MM

PERIDOTITE

OCCURS IN DIKES AND SILLS

- **COLOR** dark green to black • **GRAIN SIZE** 2–5 mm
- **MAJOR MINERALS** olivine, pyroxene, hornblende
- **MINOR MINERALS** chromite, garnet, magnetite, spinel
- **TEXTURE** medium-to-coarse crystals; some rocks have a spotted appearance that comes from larger crystals of garnet

Peridotite is a dark, coarse-grained, intrusive-igneous rock that forms much of Earth's upper mantle. It's so deep underground that it takes a volcanic eruption or other major geological event to move it toward Earth's surface.

MEDIUM-TO-COARSE CRYSTALS

GREEN WHEN FRESH; MEDIUM TO DARK BROWN WHEN WEATHERED

DUNITE

GREEN WHEN FRESH; TURNS BROWN OVER TIME

- COLOR **light green to yellowish green**
- GRAIN SIZE **2–5 mm** • MAJOR MINERALS **olivine, pyroxene, hornblende** • MINOR MINERALS **chromite, biotite, magnetite, spinel** • TEXTURE **medium-to-coarse crystals; some rocks have a spotted appearance from olivine crystals within**

Dunite is an uncommon form of peridotite, made almost entirely of the mineral olivine. Dunite usually forms sills, which are horizontal layers of igneous rock. Most dunite forms in Earth's upper mantle. It can become exposed on the Earth's surface because of the movement of Earth's plates or as chunks of rock ejected in volcanic eruptions. Dunite appears green when freshly exposed on Earth's surface. Over time, the rock is weathered and turns brown.

MEDIUM-TO-COARSE-GRAINED ROCK

OCCURS IN LAYERS CALLED SILLS

NAME GAME

Dunite is named after Dun Mountain in New Zealand. The dunite rocks on this mountain were once part of the ocean floor.

OCCURS AS FUNNEL-SHAPED STRUCTURES, OR PIPES

COARSE TEXTURE

DARK ROCK

be a ROCK HOUND!

In 1869, a massive diamond—83.5 carats!—called the "Star of South Africa" was discovered in kimberlite rock in South Africa.

KIMBERLITE

- COLOR **dark gray** • GRAIN SIZE **2–5 mm**
- MAJOR MINERALS **mica, olivine, pyroxene, garnet, diopside**
- MINOR MINERALS **ilmenite, diamond, calcite, rutile, magnetite**
- TEXTURE **generally has large crystals**

Kimberlite is a dark-gray intrusive-igneous rock with grains that vary in size. Before it forms, peridotite rock in Earth's upper mantle is heated and squeezed until some of it melts. Eventually, this molten rock, or magma, moves toward Earth's surface, where it occurs as funnel-shaped structures called pipes. As it travels, it picks up fragments—including diamonds. Then it cools and solidifies into kimberlite.

SLATE

- COLOR gray or greenish ○ GRAIN SIZE less than 0.1 mm
- MAJOR MINERALS mica, quartz, feldspar ○ MINOR MINERALS pyrite, graphite ○ TEXTURE can split into thin sheets or plates, giving it a layered appearance

Slate is a metamorphic rock. It forms when two types of sedimentary rocks—shale and mudstone—are subject to low heat and pressure beneath Earth's surface. Over millions of years, the clay minerals in these rocks are changed into mica minerals. The result is slate. Slate has a layered appearance that is caused by heat and pressure exerted on the rock.

SPOTTED SLATE

Spotted slate is a type of slate that's characterized by light and dark spots. These spots are usually crystals of minerals such as biotite and andalusite.

EXPERT'S CIRCLE

USUALLY GRAY OR GREENISH

10s spotters

FINE-GRAINED ROCK WITH MICROSCOPIC CRYSTALS THAT CAN SPLIT INTO THIN SHEETS OR PLATES

DIG THiS!

Make your own metamorphic rock! For an idea of how different rocks can be altered to form a metamorphic rock, try this sweet activity:

- Grab a handful of different chocolate candies, such as M&M'S, chocolate chips, and peanut-butter cups. These are your "rocks."
- Throw your rock candy into a small pot. Use a hair dryer on high to soften them, but not completely melt them. (If that's not working, ask an adult to help you place the pot on the stove over low heat to soften them.)
- Scrape the candy onto a sheet of wax paper. Place a second sheet of wax paper over the candy. Then, using your hands, press down on the candy.
- Remove the top sheet of wax paper and observe the metamorphic rock you just created. How is this slab different from the original candy "rocks"?

PHYLLITE

FINE-GRAINED ROCK

* COLOR dark green or gray * GRAIN SIZE less than 0.1 mm
* MAJOR MINERALS quartz, feldspar, chlorite, muscovite mica, graphite * MINOR MINERALS tourmaline, andalusite, biotite, staurolite * TEXTURE foliated, or layered

Phyllite is a metamorphic rock. It has a shiny appearance that's caused by mica crystals in the rock. Phyllite forms when fine-grained sedimentary rocks, such as shale and mudstone, are buried beneath Earth's surface. There, the rocks are altered by increased pressure and temperature. First, the rocks are changed into slate. After more time, they change into phyllite. Phyllite is related to slate, but has a much glossier sheen.

10s spotters

OFTEN DARK GREEN OR GRAY

TENDS TO SPLIT INTO SHEETS; GLOSSIER SHEEN THAN SLATE

be a ROCK HOUND!

The mica crystals in phyllite are aligned in a parallel fashion. This causes the rock to split into thick sheets.

10s spotters

LIGHT-COLORED, SWIRLY BANDS CAUSED BY PARTIAL MELTING

→ LOOK FOR THIS
Migmatites are often used as decorative stones.

MIGMATITE

* COLOR banded light and dark gray, pink, white
* GRAIN SIZE 2–5 mm * MAJOR MINERALS quartz, feldspar, mica
* MINOR MINERALS various * TEXTURE foliated, or layered; also banded

Migmatites are metamorphic rocks that also include igneous rocks in them. How is this possible? Most migmatites form when a metamorphic rock, such as gneiss, is subject to high heat and pressure in Earth's crust. As a result, the rock partly melts. This molten portion of the rock eventually cools into igneous rock that mixes with the unmelted metamorphic part of the rock. The result is migmatite.

SCHIST

- COLOR **gray or greenish** • GRAIN SIZE **less than 0.1 mm**
- MAJOR MINERALS **mica, quartz, feldspar**
- MINOR MINERALS **pyrite, graphite** • TEXTURE **can split into thin sheets or plates, giving it a layered appearance**

Schist is a common metamorphic rock that's formed from fine-grained sedimentary rocks, such as shale and mudstone. Over time, as they are continuously heated and squeezed, the rocks form slate, then phyllite, and eventually schist. Schist has a flaky appearance that's caused by large mica crystals in the rock. The minerals are plate-like and arranged in a parallel pattern. This arrangement causes schist to split into fine layers. Other major minerals present in the rock include quartz and feldspar.

MICA SCHIST

There are many varieties of schist—each is named for the dominant mineral in the rock. One such variety is mica schist, which contains muscovite mica. Large muscovite mica crystals that form in the rock reflect light. This gives mica schist a shiny luster.

EXPERT'S CIRCLE

FLAKY APPEARANCE

10s Spotters

LARGE, PLATE-LIKE MICA CRYSTALS ARRANGED IN PARALLEL FASHION

→ LOOK FOR THIS

The type of minerals that occur in schist depend on the conditions in which the rock formed. When schist forms under very high pressure and temperatures, garnet can occur. You can identify garnet crystals by their deep red color.

GNEISS

- COLOR **gray, pink, multicolored**
- GRAIN SIZE **2–5 mm**
- MAJOR MINERALS **quartz, feldspar**
- MINOR MINERALS **biotite, hornblende, garnet, staurolite** • TEXTURE **foliated, or banded, with crystalline minerals**

Gneiss (pronounced "nice") is a metamorphic rock that makes up the core of many mountain ranges. It forms when rocks rich in quartz and/or feldspar are placed under great pressure and temperature deep in Earth's crust. These "parent rocks" that form gneiss may be either igneous or sedimentary.

BANDS OF GRAY, PINK, OR MULTICOLORED CRYSTALS

IRREGULAR, PARALLEL BANDS OF COARSE CRYSTALS

AUGEN GNEISS

Augen gneiss is a type of gneiss that has eye-shaped spots. These "eyes," or augens, are actually large mineral crystals in the rock.

EXPERT'S CIRCLE

Joke: What happens to the sedimentary rock when the pressure is on?

Answer: He turns into Mr. Gneiss guy.

METAMORPHIC   135

AMPHIBOLITE

- COLOR gray, black, greenish • GRAIN SIZE 2–5 mm
- MAJOR MINERALS hornblende, tremolite, actinolite
- MINOR MINERALS feldspar, calcite, garnet, pyroxene
- TEXTURE foliated, or layered; has a clear crystal structure

An amphibolite is a dark-colored metamorphic rock that has large crystals and a high concentration of amphiboles present, including black hornblende as well as tremolite and actinolite. Most amphibolites form when dark igneous rocks like basalt and gabbro experience high pressure and temperature. Amphibolites may also form from clay-rich sedimentary rocks, such as marl and graywacke.

WEATHERED APPEARANCE WHEN EXPOSED ON EARTH'S SURFACE

DARK ROCK OFTEN FOUND WITH LIGHTER-COLORED SCHIST AND GNEISS

→ LOOK FOR THIS
Amphibolites are often used as building stone, particularly as an aggregate in the construction of roads. But they may also be used on the exterior of buildings when they are cut and polished.

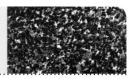

HORNFELS

- COLOR dark gray, brown, greenish, reddish
- GRAIN SIZE less than 0.1 mm • MAJOR MINERALS hornblende, plagioclase, andalusite, and others • MINOR MINERALS magnetite, apatite, titanite • TEXTURE crystal structure

Hornfels is a fine-grained metamorphic rock. It is usually dark, dense, and hard to break. Hornfels is formed from a process called contact metamorphism. During this process, heat and steam from a pool of magma heat the surrounding rocks. The high temperature transforms these surrounding rocks into hornfels.

DARK, DENSE COLOR

APPEARS SIMILAR TO BASALT BUT IS MUCH HARDER

MARBLE

- **COLOR** white, pink • **GRAIN SIZE** up to 2 cm
- **MAJOR MINERAL** calcite • **MINOR MINERALS** diopsite, tremolite, actinolite, dolomite • **TEXTURE** composed of interlocking crystals

Marble is a metamorphic rock that often occurs in large masses that are several hundred feet thick. Marble forms when limestone or dolomite is transformed by heat and pressure. As the calcite in limestone becomes heated, it recrystallizes. This means that a new crystal structure is created. The crystals start out very small, but over time, grow much larger and interlock. The final result is marble. The rock usually occurs in regions where metamorphic rocks are common.

MAY BE WHITE OR PINK

TYPICALLY OCCURS WITH GNEISS AND MICA SCHISTS, WHERE METAMORPHIC ROCKS ARE COMMON

→ LOOK FOR THIS

Tuckahoe is a type of marble that's found in parts of the U.S. states of New York and Connecticut. Depending on the impurities that are present, Tuckahoe marble can vary in color, ranging from light green and light gray to bluish white and brilliant white. During the 1800s, Tuckahoe marble was used to create many buildings and structures, including the Washington Memorial Arch in New York, New York, below.

SKARN

- COLOR **various** • GRAIN SIZE **up to 20 mm**
- MAJOR MINERAL **calcite** • MINOR MINERALS **garnet, forsterite, serpentine, wollastonite** • TEXTURE **crystallized minerals—fine, medium, or coarse—that often form bands**

Skarn is a type of metamorphic rock with fine, medium, or coarse grains. Sometimes, the grains are arranged in bands or in a radiating, or fanlike, manner. Skarn forms when rocks such as limestone and dolomite come in contact with hot, silica-rich water beneath Earth's surface. The water reacts with the rocks to produce new minerals, such as diopside and tremolite, in addition to other calcium, magnesium, and carbonate minerals.

MAY HAVE A BANDED APPEARANCE

OCCURS BETWEEN MARBLE AND INTRUSIVE-IGNEOUS ROCKS

be a ROCK HOUND!

Skarn can be the host rock for metallic ores of copper, lead, zinc, and gold.

SOAPSTONE

- COLOR **white, green, brown, black** • GRAIN SIZE **less than 0.1 mm**
- MAJOR MINERAL **talc** • MINOR MINERALS **chlorite, magnesite**
- TEXTURE **usually isn't foliated, or layered**

Soapstone is a fine-textured metamorphic rock consisting mostly of the mineral talc. This makes soapstone soft and easy to carve. For thousands of years, bowls, molds for spears, and art objects have been made from it. It usually forms when serpentinite is altered by heat and pressure beneath Earth's surface.

FEELS "SOAPY" TO THE TOUCH

CAN BE SCRATCHED WITH A FINGERNAIL; HAS A GREASY LUSTER

→ LOOK FOR THIS

The Christ the Redeemer Statue, which stands on top of a mountain in Rio de Janeiro, Brazil, is made partly of soapstone. The statue is considered one of the seven modern wonders of the world.

QUARTZITE

- COLOR often white or gray, but can be a variety of colors ○ GRAIN SIZE 2–5 mm ○ MAJOR MINERAL quartz
- MINOR MINERALS mica, kyanite, sillimanite
- TEXTURE composed of interlocking crystals

Quartzite is a dense, hard metamorphic rock that's made almost entirely of quartz. It forms from sandstone or chert rock that is rich in quartz. During metamorphosis, the quartz grains in the rock are heated and squeezed together until they form new, interlocking crystals. The result is metamorphic quartzite. Don't confuse it with quartz sandstone—that's a sedimentary rock made of rounded quartz grains cemented together.

METAMORPHIC QUARTZITE IS A HARD ROCK WITH A SUGARY APPEARANCE.

INTERLOCKING CRYSTALS; USUALLY GRAY OR WHITE

→ LOOK FOR THIS
Crushed quartzite is used primarily in road construction.

SERPENTINITE

- COLOR ranges in color from yellow-green to black, but is often green ○ GRAIN SIZE less than 0.1 mm ○ MAJOR MINERAL serpentine
- MINOR MINERALS chromite, magnetite, talc ○ TEXTURE not foliated, or layered

Serpentinite is a pretty metamorphic rock that forms as a result of metamorphic changes across a wide region. It often has irregular bands of color that range from yellow-green to black. Serpentinite forms after water comes in contact with rocks that are rich in olivine, such as peridotite.

BRITTLE; FEELS GREASY

OFTEN HAS COLORED STREAKS

be a ROCK HOUND!

Serpentine is formed as water continues the process it started in forming serpentinite. The water continues altering the olivine-rich rock into other minerals, such as magnetite, brucite, and serpentine. Serpentine is green in color and sometimes sold as jade.

ECLOGITE

- COLOR **red and green** · GRAIN SIZE **2–5 mm**
- MAJOR MINERALS **pyroxene, garnet** · MINOR MINERALS **kyanite, quartz, olivine, diopside** · TEXTURE **crystallized minerals may be in bands or evenly distributed in the rock**

Eclogites are striking red-and-green metamorphic rocks. Their colors come from the presence of red garnet and green pyroxene. Eclogite forms when some igneous or metamorphic rocks are exposed to extremely high pressure and temperatures deep beneath Earth's surface. Eclogites can be found as fragments in igneous rocks or as wide blocks in metamorphic rocks. They occur in western parts of North America.

RED-AND-GREEN COLOR

CRYSTALLIZED MINERALS THROUGHOUT ROCK

→ LOOK FOR THIS
On rare occasion, diamonds have occurred in eclogite. This happens when carbon is present during metamorphosis.

STREAKS OR RODLIKE STRUCTURES, PRODUCED BY THE STRETCHING OF MINERAL GRAINS THAT MAKE UP THE ROCK

MYLONITE

- COLOR **varies** · GRAIN SIZE **less than 2 mm**
- MAJOR MINERALS **varies** · MINOR MINERALS **varies**
- TEXTURE **has streaks or rodlike structures**

Mylonite is a metamorphic rock with very fine grains. It is formed by the movement of rocks along a fault, or break, in Earth's crust. In some cases, these rocks break as they move. Other times, they stretch and bend. When the latter happens, many of the minerals that make up the rocks are stretched. The result is mylonite.

be a ROCK HOUND!

Not all minerals in mylonite are stretched into tiny grains. Minerals such as quartz and feldspar can often resist being stretched. As a result, they appear as larger grains in the rock.

SANDSTONE

- COLOR generally light brown to red
- GRAIN SIZE 0.1 to 2 mm
- MAJOR MINERALS quartz is often the most common mineral, but can vary
- MINOR MINERALS cementing agents include silica, calcium carbonate, and iron oxides
- ORGANIC MATTER may contain fossilized invertebrates, vertebrates, plants
- STRUCTURE often has sand-size grains; can occur in beds, or layers

Sandstone is a very common sedimentary rock. It's made of sand-size particles held together by natural cement. These particles can be a blend of minerals, rock fragments, and organic matter that have been weathered and reduced to tiny grains. The grains are then transported by wind, water, or ice to basins, or depressions, in Earth's crust, where sediment collects and is compacted and cemented over time into rock. The White House in Washington, D.C.—home to the U.S. president—is made of sandstone that's painted white. It's from a Virginia quarry.

BROWNSTONE

Brownstone is a coarse, reddish brown sandstone. It's often composed of sediments made of feldspar, quartz, and some mica. Brownstone was used to build homes in the United States after the Civil War.

EXPERT'S CIRCLE

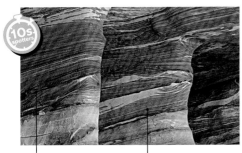

COMPOSED OF SAND-SIZE PARTICLES

OCCURS IN LAYERS CALLED BEDS

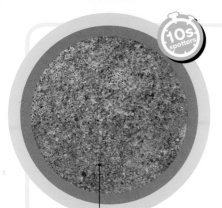

CONTAINS FELDSPAR GRAINS THAT ARE USUALLY PINK AND ANGULAR

ARKOSE

- COLOR pinkish, pale gray ○ GRAIN SIZE 0.1–2 mm
- MAJOR MINERALS quartz, feldspar ○ MINOR MINERAL mica
- ORGANIC MATTER rare ○ STRUCTURE can occur in thick or thin beds

Arkose is a type of sandstone with coarse grains usually cemented together with calcite. At least 25 percent of arkose is made of feldspar. Quartz, small amounts of mica, and rock fragments are also present. Since feldspar tends to weather quickly, it doesn't last long. So most arkose samples that you find are young compared to other rocks. Arkose is usually located near the source from which the feldspar was shed. These sources usually include granite from mountains and high, hilly lands. Arkose is especially common along the Rocky Mountains of North America.

be a ROCK HOUND!

Uluru, also known as Ayers Rock, in Australia, is made of arkose. The rock was formed more than 500 million years ago. It is located in a dry region of Australia. In this climate, feldspar breaks down very slowly.

TYPICALLY DARK

MADE OF GRAINS THAT VARY IN SIZE AND SHAPE

GRAYWACKE

- COLOR varies ○ GRAIN SIZE less than 2 mm ○ MAJOR MINERALS varies
- MINOR MINERALS varies ○ ORGANIC MATTER rare ○ TEXTURE has streaks or rodlike structures

Graywacke is a type of sandstone with grains that vary in size. They range from fine-grained clay and mud particles to large, angular rock fragments. Graywacke is formed when strong water currents carry sediments down a slope and then deposit them in a basin. Over time, the layers of sediments are pressed together to form graywacke.

be a ROCK HOUND!

Ancient Egyptians sometimes used graywacke to carve sculptures.

CONGLOMERATE

○ COLOR **varies** ○ GRAIN SIZE **ranges from 2 mm to several centimeters** ○ MAJOR MINERALS **any hard mineral** ○ MINOR MINERALS **any** ○ ORGANIC MATTER **rare** ○ STRUCTURE **massive or can occur in thick beds**

A conglomerate is a sedimentary rock made of rounded particles that are cemented together. Many of the particles are larger than 2 millimeters in diameter and can include almost anything from river pebbles to boulder fragments. This rock either contains many different particles that vary in size or the same type of particles that are about the same size. Conglomerate is formed when these particles are carried by water, landslides, or glaciers and then deposited and buried. Over time, pressure from overlying material causes the particles to become a solid rock.

10s spotters

OFTEN OCCURS BETWEEN SHALE AND SANDSTONE BEDS

VISIBLE PARTICLES, FROM PEBBLES TO ROCK PIECES

BRECCIA

Like conglomerate, breccia is a sedimentary rock that's made of different particles that are larger than 2 millimeters in diameter. The big difference between the two rocks is that the particles in conglomerate are more rounded, while those in breccia are angular. That angular shape suggests that the particles weren't carried very far. The longer particles are carried, the more worn and rounded they become.

EXPERT'S CIRCLE

be a ROCK HOUND!

In 2012, a NASA robot on Mars discovered what appears to be conglomerate. The particles within the rock were large and rounded, suggesting that water moved them and tumbled them into a rounded shape. This gives us evidence that water once flowed on Mars.

ROCK STARS:
Dinosaur Bones

TRICERATOPS

Triceratops boasted two large horns and a neck frill that spanned six feet (1.8 m). In spite of its menacing appearance, this dinosaur was a plant-eater and likely used its horns and frill to defend itself from attackers. The first *Triceratops* was discovered in Denver, Colorado, U.S.A.

ALLOSAURUS

More than 10,000 *Allosaurus* bones have been discovered in the U.S. state of Utah. This meat-eating dinosaur had 70 thick, sharp teeth for tearing into its prey. In addition, its jawbones were very flexible, allowing the dinosaur to hold large chunks of meat in its mouth.

STEGOSAURUS

Stegosaurus was a plant-eating dinosaur that had two rows of bony plates along its back. This was a fairly large dinosaur, measuring about the length of a bus. The most complete *Stegosaurus* skeleton ever found was in the U.S. state of Wyoming.

Dinosaur Fossil Finds

Many dinosaur fossils have been discovered in North America. Those you see here are all from western U.S. states. The fossils are usually found in dry areas with sedimentary rocks that formed 225 to 65.5 million years ago. This was the Mesozoic Era, or the "age of dinosaurs." Scientists who study dinosaur remains are called paleontologists.

TYRANNOSAURUS REX

Tyrannosaurus rex was a feared meat-eater, with teeth the size of bananas! The best preserved *T. rex* fossil was found in South Dakota, U.S.A., near the city of Faith. The *T. rex* was nicknamed "Sue," after Sue Hendrickson, the paleontologist who discovered the fossil.

CAMARASAURUS

Paleontologists found these exposed bones of *Camarasaurus*—a plant-eating dinosaur—at Carnegie Dinosaur Quarry in Utah, U.S.A.

SHALE

- COLOR **varies** • GRAIN SIZE **less than 0.1 mm**
- MAJOR MINERALS **clays, quartz, calcite**
- MINOR MINERALS **pyrite, iron oxides, feldspars**
- ORGANIC MATTER: **may contain fossilized invertebrates, vertebrates, plants** • STRUCTURE: **occurs in beds**

Shale is a common sedimentary rock with grains that are smaller than those of sand and are invisible to the naked eye. It is composed mainly of clay and silt. Shale forms when clay and silt sediments are deposited by slow-moving waters onto the ocean floor, shallow sea basins, and river flood-plains. As more sediment gets deposited, the particles underneath become tightly packed. Eventually, they become a dense, solid rock.

TINY GRAINS INVISIBLE TO THE NAKED EYE

FORMS IN LAYERS, WHICH CAN SPLIT INTO THIN PIECES

be a ROCK HOUND !

The Burgess Shale is a rock formation in Canada that's more than 500 million years old. Fossils of more than 200 different living things have been found in this formation.

FINE-GRAINED

MARL

- COLOR **varies** • GRAIN SIZE **less than 0.1 mm** • MAJOR MINERALS **clays, calcite** • MINOR MINERALS **glauconite, hematite** • ORGANIC MATTER **invertebrates, vertebrates, plants** • STRUCTURE **often occurs in thin beds, or layers**

Marl is a group of fine-grained sedi-mentary rocks that form in shallow freshwater or seawater. Marls are usually made of clay minerals cemented together with calcium carbonate. The calcium car-bonate may come from shell fragments of water organisms, or it can be deposited by algae. When the clay minerals and calcium carbonate are compacted together over time, they form marl. Because of its calcium-carbonate content, it reacts with acid.

FORMS IN SHALLOW FRESHWATER OR SEAWATER

USUALLY BREAKS INTO BLOCKS OR ROUNDED NODULES

CHERT

- COLOR white, gray, brown, yellow, black
- GRAIN SIZE none • MAJOR MINERAL chalcedony
- MINOR MINERALS none • ORGANIC MATTER invertebrates, plants • STRUCTURE occurs in layers or nodules

Chert is a hard sedimentary rock that occurs in layers or rounded masses called nodules. Chert forms from the precipitation of silica in a marine environment. The silica often comes from the skeletal remains of tiny marine organisms that have fallen to the ocean floor. Here, they dissolve and then recrystallize as superfine quartz. The tiny crystals are visible only under a microscope. Together they make up chert.

OCCURS IN LAYERS OR NODULES IN FINE-GRAINED LIMESTONE AND CHALK

MAY BE WHITE, YELLOW, OR DARKER COLORS

→ LOOK FOR THIS

"Flint" is the name given to white and gray varieties of chert that occur as nodules. Flint was used by early humans to make weapons such as spear points.

DOLOMITE ROCK

- COLOR gray to yellowish gray; yellowish beige or brown when weathered • GRAIN SIZE none • MAJOR MINERAL dolomite
- MINOR MINERAL calcite • ORGANIC MATTER invertebrates
- STRUCTURE occurs as massive layers, or as thin layers in limestone

Dolomite is a sedimentary rock. It forms when another sedimentary rock, limestone, alters or changes. The change happens when magnesium-rich water flows into the limestone. The water replaces the limestone's calcium carbonate with the mineral dolomite. Dolomite rock looks like limestone, but it turns yellowish beige or brown when it weathers.

ROCK IS OFTEN GRAY, BUT MAY TURN YELLOW WHEN WEATHERED

CAN OCCUR AS MASSIVE LAYERS, OR AS THIN LAYERS IN LIMESTONE

→ LOOK FOR THIS

Dolomite is rich in magnesium and has many industrial uses: It's an ingredient in concrete and fertilizers. It's also a "flux." That's a material that melts easily and is used to take impurities out of iron.

LIMESTONE

- COLOR white, gray, pink
- GRAIN SIZE usually none
- MAJOR MINERAL calcite
- MINOR MINERALS aragonite, dolomite, siderite, quartz, pyrite
- ORGANIC MATTER marine and freshwater invertebrates
- STRUCTURE occurs as thick or thin beds

Limestone is a light-colored sedimentary rock that usually forms in warm, shallow marine waters. The rock is made mostly of calcium carbonate—a chemical compound, which in this case takes the form of calcite. Often, this compound comes from organisms in the water. Other times, it may be deposited from the water itself. Limestone deposits can occur as thick or thin beds and cover vast areas. In dry regions, they can even form cliffs.

TRAVERTINE

Travertine is limestone that usually forms when mineral springs evaporate and deposit calcium carbonate. It's sometimes called Mexican onyx or Egyptian alabaster. Travertine limestone forms in a way similar to the limestone that forms stalactites, which look like stone icicles hanging from the roof of a cave. But travertine is less coarse-grained and has a higher polish than limestone.

EXPERT'S CIRCLE

FINE-TO-MEDIUM–GRAINED ROCK

10s. spotters

FIZZES WHEN IN CONTACT WITH ACID

be a ROCK HOUND!

The peak of Mount Everest—the world's tallest mountain—is made from limestone that formed in a marine environment. Millions of years ago, the limestone rested on the seafloor. But as the mountain formed, the rock was pushed upward, thousands of feet above the water's surface.

ROCK GYPSUM

- COLOR **white, gray, pink** • GRAIN SIZE **fine-to-medium–grained crystals** • MAJOR MINERAL **gypsum**
- MINOR MINERAL **anhydrite** • ORGANIC MATTER **none**
- STRUCTURE **occurs in thin to thick beds**

Rock gypsum is a fine-to-medium–grained sedimentary rock. It forms in bodies of salt water such as oceans. As the salt water evaporates, crystals of the mineral gypsum are left behind. Over time, these gypsum deposits accumulate and form rock gypsum. This rock generally occurs in massive beds that range in thickness from a few inches to several feet.

SOFT ROCK WITH FINE-GRAINED CRYSTALS

OCCURS IN DISTINCT LAYERS OR BEDS

OFTEN FOUND WITH BEDS OF SHALE, LIMESTONE, AND ROCK SALT

→ LOOK FOR THIS

In dry regions, rock gypsum is resistant to erosion, the process in which rock is worn away and moved elsewhere. But in damp areas, rock gypsum is easily eroded.

ROCK SALT

- COLOR **white, pinkish, gray, yellowish** • GRAIN SIZE **varies from microscopic to several inches, depending on the size of the crystals** • MAJOR MINERAL **halite** • MINOR MINERAL **halite**
- ORGANIC MATTER **none** • STRUCTURE **often forms in thick beds**

Rock salt is formed from halite crystals that were deposited by seawater as it evaporated. Rock salt often occurs in thick beds deep underground. However, since rock salt is usually less dense than surrounding rocks, it tends to rise and push through overlying rock. This causes moundlike structures called salt domes to form. The domes can vary in size, but some are up to six miles (10 km) in diameter!

BRITTLE; FEELS GREASY

OFTEN HAS COLORED STREAKS

be a ROCK HOUND!

More than 500 salt domes have been discovered under the Gulf of Mexico seafloor.

COAL

- COLOR black • GRAIN SIZE microscopic
- MAJOR MINERALS none • MINOR MINERALS plants
- ORGANIC MATTER may have plant fossils in it
- STRUCTURE occurs in layers

Coal is a sedimentary rock used as a source of energy. It is the only rock that burns. It is formed when thick layers of dead plants build up in a swampy environment. There is little oxygen in this environment, so the plants don't decay quickly. Eventually, they are covered by other sediments and are compacted. Over millions of years, the plant pieces undergo physical and chemical changes until they are transformed into coal. This kind of coal is called bituminous. Another kind of coal, anthracite, is a metamorphic rock.

EXPERT'S CIRCLE

LIGNITE

Lignite, also a sedimentary rock, is a brown-black coal that looks very different from the bituminous coal specimen shown above. In lignite, plant materials have been transformed into a very soft rock, but are still somewhat recognizable. By contrast, plant features can rarely be seen in bituminous coal.

DULL BLACK COLOR

10s spotters

BITUMINOUS COAL IS A SOFT, LIGHTWEIGHT ROCK.

be a ROCK HOUND!

Coal is called a fossil fuel because it's made from the preserved remains, or fossils, of plants. It takes millions of years for the remains to build up and for coal to form. Coal is a nonrenewable resource. This means that if all the coal in the ground is used up, we can't make more in our lifetime.

COQUINA

- COLOR **tan** • GRAIN SIZE **coarse shell fragments**
- MAJOR MINERAL **aragonite** • MINOR MINERALS **silicate minerals, especially quartz** • ORGANIC MATTER **invertebrates** • STRUCTURE **often found in beds**

Coquina is a type of limestone made mostly of shell fragments from marine creatures, such as clams and oysters. The fragments are loosely cemented together by calcite. The rock is formed in shallow water near beaches, where waves batter shells into small fragments. Coquina can be found in many places around the world, but the most well-known occurrences are in the U.S. state of Florida.

LOOSELY CEMENTED SHELL FRAGMENTS

TAN COLOR

be a ROCK HOUND!

Coquina was used to build Fort San Marcos, in St. Augustine, Florida, U.S.A., in the 1600s. During battles, enemy cannonballs struck the wall. Instead of shattering it, they bounced off or got stuck in it!

CHALK

- COLOR **usually white or gray** • GRAIN SIZE **very small—less than 0.1 mm** • MAJOR MINERAL **calcite** • MINOR MINERALS **quartz and clays** • ORGANIC MATTER **tiny invertebrate fossils may be present** • STRUCTURE **often found in beds**

Chalk is a type of limestone made from the tiny skeletons of ancient marine creatures that were deposited on the seafloor millions of years ago. There the skeletons mixed with mud and hardened into chalk deposits. These were pushed upward by geological forces. Some southern U.S. states have huge chalk deposits.

SOFT LIMESTONE WITH A FINE TEXTURE

WHITE OR LIGHT GRAY

→ LOOK FOR THIS

Natural chalk was first used for drawing more than 10,000 years ago. Most "chalk" used today for drawing is a human-made substance.

Quick ID

CALLING ALL ROCK HOUNDS!

Rocks are all around you, whether you're in your backyard or on a family vacation to a national park. These profiles will help you quickly identify some key rocks. Be sure to check out their full information on the pages listed with them. Grab your pad and pencil to make field notes, so you'll find them again on your next rock-hunting adventure.

BASALT – 120

RHYOLITE – 121

ANDESITE – 123

SCORIA – 124

OBSIDIAN – 124

GRANITE – 125

GRANITE PEGMATITE – 126

SLATE – 132

PHYLLITE - 133

SCHIST – 134

GNEISS – 135

AMPHIBOLITE – 136

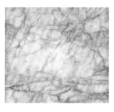

MARBLE – 137

SOAPSTONE – 138

QUARTZITE – 139

SANDSTONE – 141

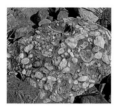

CONGLOMERATE – 143

SHALE – 146

CHERT – 147

LIMESTONE – 148

ROCK GYPSUM – 149

ROCK SALT – 149

COAL – 150

COQUINA - 151

Glossary

ALTERATION PRODUCT: A new mineral that's created when an existing mineral goes through a process of change, or alteration

ATOM: The smallest unit of a substance that still has the properties of that substance

BED: A layer of rock

BOTRYOIDAL: Bubble-shaped or grape-shaped

BRILLIANT: The shiniest luster a mineral can have

CHEMICAL WEATHERING: The process of rocks being broken down by chemical reactions with water, oxygen, and carbon dioxide, or acids

CLEAVAGE: The way a mineral breaks or splits naturally

COLUMNAR: Shaped like a column

COMPOUND: A substance formed of the atoms of two or more elements

CONGLOMERATE: A coarse-grained sedimentary rock with both large and small grains

CRUST: The outermost layer of Earth

CRYSTAL: The form a mineral takes, which is made by a repeating pattern of atoms and molecules

DIKE: A sheet of rock formed in the fracture of another rock

DODECAHEDRON: A three-dimensional structure with 12 faces

DULL: The least shiny luster a mineral can have

EROSION: The process in which sediment is moved from one place to another

FLUORESCENT: The property of a mineral to glow under ultraviolet light

FRACTURE: A break in the surface of a mineral that is different from the cleavage, which is the main way a mineral splits

GEM: A cut stone valued for its color, rarity, texture, or clarity. Gems are often worn in jewelry.

GEODE: A hollow nodule (a rounded mass) that's often lined with crystals

HABIT: The shape of a mineral's crystal

HARDNESS: The measure of how resistant a mineral is to being scratched

HEXAGONAL: A six-sided shape

HYDROTHERMAL REPLACEMENT DEPOSIT: A mineral deposit left by hot waters circulating under Earth's crust. The action replaces existing rock with the new minerals, creating new rock.

HYDROTHERMAL VEIN: A rock fracture in which minerals have been deposited by fluids circulating deep within Earth's crust

IGNEOUS ROCK: A rock formed by the cooling and solidifying of magma or lava as it moves toward Earth's surface

LAVA: Molten rock on Earth's surface

LUSTER: The shine of a mineral caused by reflected light

MAGMA: Hot molten rock beneath Earth's surface

MAJOR MINERAL: A mineral that is a large part of a rock's makeup

MANTLE: The layer of rock beneath Earth's crust

MASSIVE: A mineral form having no definite shape

METAL: An element that conducts heat and electricity well

METAMORPHIC ROCK: A rock changed by heat and/or pressure

MINERAL: A natural, nonliving solid substance that has a definite chemical composition and set crystal structure

MINOR MINERAL: A mineral that is only a small part of a rock's makeup

NODULES: Small, irregularly rounded knots or masses

OCTAHEDRON: A three-dimensional figure composed of eight equilateral triangles

ORB: A ball-like shape

ORGANIC: Made up of materials that were once living

PALEOLITHIC AGE: The early part of the Stone Age, when stone instruments were used, starting about 2.6 million years ago

PISOLITIC: Made up of many grains, each no larger than the size of a pea

PLATE: A giant slab of rock that makes up Earth's crust

PLATY: A plate-like shape: flattened and thin

PRECIPITATE: A solid deposit that comes from a solution. For instance, the mineral aragonite is deposited by warm ocean waters.

PRISM: An element with flat surfaces that refract, or bend, light

QUARRY: A deep pit from which rock is mined

RESINOUS: A smooth, not shiny, luster

RHOMBOHEDRON: A prism with six faces. Each face is made up of a rhombus, or a four-sided shape

SEDIMENTARY ROCK: Rock formed at or near Earth's surface from sediment that piled up and was cemented together

STALACTITE: An icicle-shaped rock formed by mineral-rich water dripping from the ceiling of a cave

STONE AGE: The earliest part of history, when people used stone tools, starting 2.6 million years ago

STRIATIONS: A series of lines or ridges

TABULAR: Tablet-shaped

TWINNED CRYSTALS: Crystal growths that are mirror images of one another—like identical twins

VEINS: Sheetlike bodies of crystallized minerals

VESICLE: A small, round cavity

WEATHERING: Process of rocks crumbling due to rain, wind, or other atmospheric conditions

Photo Credits

Find Out More

Want to find out even more about rocks and minerals? Check out these books, websites, videos, and apps. Be sure to ask an adult to help you search the Web to find the sites below.

BOOKS

Furgang, Kathy. *Everything Volcanoes and Earthquakes: Earthshaking Photos, Facts, and Fun!* National Geographic Kids, 2013.

Green, Dan. *Scholastic Discover More: Rocks and Minerals.* Scholastic, 2013.

Pocket Genius: Rocks and Minerals. Dorling Kindersley Publishing, 2012.

Smithsonian: Dinosaur! Dorling Kindersley Publishing, 2014.

Tomecek, Steve. *Dirtmeister's Nitty Gritty Planet Earth: All About Rocks, Minerals, Fossils, Earthquakes, Volcanoes & Even Dirt!* National Geographic Kids, 2015.

————. *Everything Rocks and Minerals: Dazzling Gems of Photos and Info That Will Rock Your World.* National Geographic Kids, 2011.

WEBSITES

Collecting: Rocks and Minerals
Smithsonian Kids
smithsonianeducation.org/students/smithsonian_kids_collecting/main.html

Dinosaur Train
PBS Kids
pbskids.org/dinosaurtrain/games/fieldguide.html

The Dynamic Earth
Smithsonian National Museum of Natural History
mnh.si.edu/earth/main_frames.html

Gem-o-Matic
Scholastic Play!
scholastic.com/play/pregem.htm

Mineralogy 4 Kids
Mineralogical Society of America
mineralogy4kids.org

MSHA Kids Page: Mining Resources by State
Mine Safety and Health Administration (MSHA)
msha.gov/KIDS/MINING.HTM

National Geographic Kids: Dinosaurs
National Geographic Society
kids.nationalgeographic.com/explore/nature/dinosaurs

Ology
American Museum of Natural History
amnh.org/explore/ology/earth

One Geology Kids
National Environment Research Council
onegeology.org/extra/kids/rocks_and_minerals.html

VIDEOS

Gem Formation
National Geographic
channel.nationalgeographic.com/videos/gem-formation

Volcanoes 101
National Geographic
video.nationalgeographic.com/video/101-videos/volcanoes-101

Weathering and Erosion
Scholastic Study Jams
studyjams.scholastic.com/studyjams/jams/science/rocks-minerals-landforms/weathering-and-erosion.htm

APPS

(iOS)
Common Rocks Reference
itunes.apple.com/us/app/common-rocks-reference/id301217333?mt=8

Digger's Map—Natural Resources and Minerals
itunes.apple.com/us/app/diggers-map-natural-resources/id556478719?mt=8

Mineral Identifier
itunes.apple.com/us/app/mineral-identifier/id531342975?mt=8

(Android)
Dinosaur Hunt
play.google.com/store/apps/details?id=org.greyolltwit.dinohunt&hl=en

Key: Minerals (Earth Science)
play.google.com/store/apps/details?id=com.bim.key.mineral3&hl=en

Minerals and Crystals
play.google.com/store/apps/details?id=com.wMineral-Bookstore&hl=en

FOR TEACHERS:

Geology.com
geology.com/

Interactives: Rock Cycle
Annenberg Learner
learner.org/interactives/rockcycle

Rocks
Discovery Education
discoveryeducation.com/teachers/free-lesson-plans/rocks.cfm

USGS Education
USGS
education.usgs.gov

Index

Staff for This Book
Amy Briggs, Priyanka Sherman, *Senior Editors*
Jim Hiscott, *Art Director*
Lori Epstein, *Senior Photo Editor*
Angela Modany, *Assistant Editor*
Paige Towler, *Editorial Assistant*
Sanjida Rashid and Rachel Kenny, *Design Production Assistants*
Tammi Colleary-Loach, *Rights Clearance Manager*
Michael Cassady and Mari Robinson, *Rights Clearance Specialists*
Grace Hill, *Managing Editor*
Joan Gossett, *Senior Production Editor*
Lewis R. Bassford, *Production Manager*
Jennifer Hoff, *Manager, Production Services*
Susan Borke, *Legal and Business Affairs*

Produced by Potomac Global Media, LLC
Kevin Mulroy, *Publisher*
Barbara Brownell Grogan, *Editorial Director*
Nancy Honovich, *Author*
Stephen Tomecek, James Lucarelli, *Technical Consultants, Science Plus, Inc.*
Chris Mazzatenta, *Art Director*
David Hicks, Uliana Bazar, *Picture Editors*
Kelly S. Horvath, *Contributing Editor*
Tim Griffin, *Indexer*

Published by the National Geographic Society
Gary E. Knell, *President and CEO*
John M. Fahey, *Chairman of the Board*
Melina Gerosa Bellows, *Chief Education Officer*
Declan Moore, *Chief Media Officer*
Hector Sierra, *Senior Vice President and General Manager, Book Division*

Senior Management Team, Kids Publishing and Media: Nancy Laties Feresten, *Senior Vice President*; Erica Green, *Vice President, Editorial Director, Kids Books*; Amanda Larsen, *Design Director, Kids Books*; Julie Vosburgh Agnone, *Vice President, Operations*; Jennifer Emmett, *Vice President, Content*; Michelle Sullivan, *Vice President, Video and Digital Initiatives*; Eva Absher-Schantz, *Vice President, Visual Identity*; Rachel Buchholz, *Editor and Vice President, NG Kids magazine*; Jay Sumner, *Photo Director*; Hannah August, *Marketing Director*; R. Gary Colbert, *Production Director*

Digital
Laura Goertzel, *Manager*; Sara Zeglin, *Senior Producer*; Bianca Bowman, *Assistant Producer*; Natalie Jones, *Senior Product Manager*

The National Geographic Society is one of the world's largest nonprofit scientific and educational organizations. Founded in 1888 to "increase and diffuse geographic knowledge," the Society's mission is to inspire people to care about the planet. It reaches more than 400 million people worldwide each month through its official journal, *National Geographic*, and other magazines; National Geographic Channel; television documentaries; music; radio; films; books; DVDs; maps; exhibitions; live events; school publishing programs; interactive media; and merchandise. National Geographic has funded more than 10,000 scientific research, conservation, and exploration projects and supports an education program promoting geographic literacy.

For more information, please visit nationalgeographic.com, call 1-800-NGS LINE (647-5463), or write to the following address:

National Geographic Society
1145 17th Street N.W.
Washington, D.C. 20036-4688 U.S.A.

Visit us online at nationalgeographic.com/books

For librarians and teachers: ngchildrensbooks.org

More for kids from National Geographic: kids.nationalgeographic.com

For information about special discounts for bulk purchases, please contact National Geographic Books Special Sales: ngspecsales@ngs.org

For rights or permissions inquiries, please contact National Geographic Books Subsidiary Rights: ngbookrights@ngs.org

Trade paperback ISBN: 978-1-4263-2301-0

Reinforced library binding ISBN: 978-1-4263-2302-7

Printed in China
15/RRDS/1